I0648853

Edward James Jones

A Handbook of Phonography

Edward James Jones

A Handbook of Phonography

ISBN/EAN: 9783337399962

Printed in Europe, USA, Canada, Australia, Japan

Cover: Foto ©Thomas Meinert / pixelio.de

More available books at **www.hansebooks.com**

A

HANDBOOK of PHONOGRAPHY,

OR,

A NEW AND IMPROVED METHOD OF WRITING WORDS
ACCORDING TO THEIR SOUNDS;

BEING A COMPLETE SYSTEM OF

PHONIC SHORTHAND,

ADAPTED FOR CORRESPONDENCE,

VERBATIM REPORTING, &c.

BY EDWARD JAMES JONES.

(For eighteen years a writer of Mr. Isaac Pitman's system)

LONDON:
S. W. PARTRIDGE, 9, PATERNOSTER ROW,
MANCHESTER:
WILLIAM BREMNER, 11, MARKET STREET.
1862.

WILLIAM HORSMAN, PRINTER, MIDDLETON, NEAR MANCHESTER.

TO

SHORTHAND WRITERS IN GENERAL,

BUT PARTICULARLY TO THOSE INTERESTED IN THE PROGRESS

OF

PHONO-STENOGRAPHY,

THIS WORK IS RESPECTFULLY DEDICATED BY

THE AUTHOR

A late writer (Mr. William Cobbett), in an introduction to one of his works, remarks, that the preface of a book should inform the reader *why* the work was written, and then give any information which might be desirable or convenient for the reader to possess before commencing a more thorough perusal of the book.

The reader of this work will doubtless expect its author briefly to state the reasons which induced him to give up a system of shorthand with which he was thoroughly familiar, and to construct another in its stead.

Mr. Pitman's Phonography was laid aside on account of its author's expressed determination to adopt certain not only useless, but, at the same time, very inconvenient alterations; the "*New Word-position Scale*" in particular.* Real improvements would have been welcomed, as may be inferred from Mr. Isaac Pitman's own acknowledgment that *his* phonography owes much to the author of this system. With extensive, crude, and untested changes,—changes for the mere love of change, the writer of this work has no sympathy; he therefore preferred the pleasing labour of arranging an entirely new system, rather than undergo the annoyance and inconvenience inseparable from a *needless* lack of stability in the system he then practised.

In Mr. Pitman's system of phonography, certain details are felt

---

* Since the above was written, the correctness of the opinion held by many of the best phonographers in the country respecting the utter worthlessness of this scale has been confirmed. After advocating the superiority of this scale in the *Phonetic Journal* from July, 1861, to May, 1862, Mr. Pitman suddenly abandoned it as worse than useless, being in fact calculated to "inflict an injury on the system."

to be objectionable, both by teacher and learner. Being of opinion that a new system could be developed, free, in a great measure, from the defects referred to, and feeling a deep interest in the advancement of the Phono-Stenographic Art, the author of this "Handbook" resolved to attempt the construction of a new system, and he is happy to say with a result which is considered highly satisfactory by parties who have been very good writers and teachers of Mr. Pitman's shorthand, but who now use this in preference.

In comparing this with preceding systems, the author has selected that which he considers to be the best of them, viz., Mr. Isaac Pitman's. The leading features of the two, and points of difference, are noticed under the head of Pitman's system, in the sketch which we have given of the History of Shorthand; and at the end of the reading exercises will be found a page of our phonography, interlined with Mr. Pitman's for comparison.

Had not the author been urgently requested by many phonographic friends to publish this little volume in time for use by the winter classes of 1862-3 which they intended forming, he would have preferred to give a little more time to the general "getting up" of the work. This, however, could not be, without causing much disappointment. Considering these circumstances, it is hoped that any little imperfections in arrangement, printing, &c., will be excused; and should another edition be called for, they will be avoided.

The details of this system have been thoroughly considered, sifted, and tested by practice; and, considering that the author has had the benefit of nearly twenty years' stenographic experience, it is expected that no necessity will be found for fundamental alterations.

To those shorthand writers who have subjected this new system to the touch-stone of practice, and thus kindly assisted in developing its details, the author presents his grateful acknowledgments.

E. J. JONES.

Rhodes, Middleton,
    near Manchester.

ADVANTAGES OF SHORTHAND.

"Shorthand, on account of its great and general utility, merits a much higher rank among the arts and sciences than is generally allotted to it. Its usefulness is not confined to any particular science or profession, but is universal: it is therefore by no means unworthy the attention and study of men of genius and erudition." — *Dr. Samuel Johnson.*

.

To many minds, the very mention of the word "Shorthand" will suggest many advantages resulting therefrom. In addition to its more general application to reporting, it is highly serviceable for other purposes. Phonic Shorthand may be used with a great saving of time for correspondence between friends who practise the same system. If no such correspondence exist, even then, the art is exceedingly useful for writing drafts, or copies of longhand letters; rough-sketching matters of business, &c.

For the writing of literary compositions it is of great utility, as the matter can either be delivered from the shorthand notes, or a longhand copy written therefrom for the printer. If the compositor understand the system, a longhand transcription is unnecessary, as the types can be set up from shorthand copy. Authors, who now use shorthand, but vividly remember the time when their thoughts had to "struggle through the strait gate of the old handwriting," know well how to appreciate a system of writing which enables the pen to keep pace with, or even to outstrip the powers of composition, and saves not only many valuable thoughts which would otherwise slip, unpenned, into oblivion, but also the author's time, manual labor, and, probably, his health.

For keeping a diary, taking extracts from books, and general memoranda, a method of brief writing is, manifestly, a great convenience.

The acquirement of the pronunciation of a foreign language is rendered much more easy and certain by a knowledge of Phonic Shorthand, and for the linguist and philologist, *this* system is peculiarly adapted on account of its phonetic accuracy, and the efficient means which it provides for the easy representation of foreign sounds.

In houses of business, shorthand steps in as an economizer of time. The principal of a commercial establishment, by dictating the replies to his letters at the rate of ordinary speech to a competent Phonographer, may conduct the largest correspondence in almost a tithe of the time ordinarily required; thus saving much of his time and energy for other important duties. His shorthand clerk would afterwards write out the replies in longhand, ready for signature or posting. This use of shorthand in mercantile and railway offices is becoming growingly important, and will no doubt receive due consideration by steady and intelligent young men, of business habits; persons capable of filling such offices being, at present, comparatively few.

We here transcribe a few excellent remarks on the advantages of shorthand, penned by Mr. Gawtress,* the publisher of an improved edition of Byrom's system. These remarks have been deservedly reprinted in many shorthand works, both English and American. We may observe, that whatever can be said on the advantages of the old *a b c* methods, will apply with still greater force to a Phonetic and superior system.

" Shorthand is capable of imparting so many advantages to persons in almost every situation of life, and is of such extensive utility to society, that it is justly a matter of surprise, that it has not attracted a greater share of attention, and been more generally practised.

" In England, at least, this art may be considered a National Blessing, and thousands who look with the utmost indifference upon it, are daily reaping the fruits of its cultivation. It is scarcely necessary to mention how indispensable it is in taking minutes of public proceedings. If all the feelings of a patriot glow in our bosoms on a perusal of those eloquent

---

* It is a somewhat curious coincidence that the printer of this Handbook was, when a young man, a journeyman under Mr. Gawtress, and assisted in the printing of the work above mentioned.

speeches which are delivered in the Senate, or in those public assemblies where the people are frequently convened to exercise the birthright of Britons—we owe it to shorthand. If new fervor be added to our devotion, and an additional stimulus be imparted to our exertions as Christians, by the eloquent appeals and encouraging statements made at the anniversaries of our various religious Societies—we owe it to shorthand. If we have an opportunity, in interesting judicial cases, of examining the evidence, and learning the proceedings, with as much certainty, and nearly as much minuteness, as if we had been present on the occasion—we owe it to shorthand. In short, all those brilliant and spirit-stirring effusions which the circumstances of the present times combine to draw forth, and which the press transmits to us with such astonishing celerity, warm from the lips and instinct with the soul of the speaker, would have been entirely lost to posterity, and comparatively little known to ourselves, had it not been for the facilities afforded for their preservation by shorthand. Were the operations of those who are professionally engaged in exercising this art, to be suspended but for a single week, a blank would be left in the political and judicial history of our country, an impulse would be wanting to the public mind, and the nation would be taught to feel and acknowledge the important purposes it answers in the great business of life,

" A practical acquaintance with this art is highly favourable to the improvement of the mind, invigorating all its faculties, and drawing forth all its resources. The close attention requisite in following the voice of the speaker, induces habits of patience, perseverance, and watchfulness, which will gradually extend themselves to other pursuits and avocations, and at length inure the writer to exercise them on every occasion in life. When writing in public, it will also be absolutely necessary to distinguish and adhere to the train of thought which runs through the discourse, and to observe the modes of its connection. This will naturally have a tendency to endue the mind with quickness of apprehension, and will impart an habitual readiness and distinctness of perception, as well as a methodical simplicity of arrangement, which cannot fail to conduce greatly to mental superiority. The judgment will be strengthened, and the taste refined ; and the practitioner will, by degrees, become habituated to seize the original and leading parts of a discourse or harangue, and to reject whatever is common-place, trivial, or uninteresting.

"The *memory* is also improved by the practice of stenography. The obligation the writer is under to retain in his mind the last sentence of the speaker, at the same time that he is carefully attending to the following one, must be highly beneficial to that faculty, which, more than any other, owes its improvement to exercise. And so much are the powers of retention strengthened and expanded by this exertion, that a practical stenographer will frequently recollect more without writing, than a person unacquainted with the art could copy in the time by the use of common-hand.

"It has been justly observed, 'this science draws out all the powers of the mind;—it excites invention, improves the ingenuity, matures the judgment, and endows the retentive faculty with the superior advantages of precision, vigilance, and perseverance.'

"The *facility it affords to the acquisition of learning* ought to render it an indispensable branch in the education of youth. To be enabled to treasure up for future study the substance of lectures, sermons, &c., is an accomplishment attended with so many evident advantages that it stands in no need of recommendation. Nor is it a matter of small importance, that by this art the youthful student is furnished with an easy means of making a number of valuable extracts in the moments of leisure, and of thus laying up a stock of knowledge for his future occasions. The pursuit of this art materially contributes to improve the student in the principles of grammar and composition. While tracing the various forms of expression by which the same sentiment can be conveyed; and while endeavoring to represent, by modes of contraction, the dependence of one word upon another, he is insensibly initiated in the science of universal language, and particularly in the knowledge of his native tongue.

"The rapidity with which it enables a person to commit his own thoughts to the safety of manuscript, also renders it an object peculiarly worthy of regard. By this means many ideas which daily strike us, and which are lost before we can record them in the usual way, may be snatched from destruction, and preserved till mature deliberation can ripen and perfect them.

"In addition to these great advantages, Science and Religion are indebted to this inestimable art for the preservation of many valuable lectures and sermons, which would otherwise have been irrecoverably lost. Among the latter may be instanced those of

Whitfield, whose astonishing powers could move even infidelity itself, and extort admiration from a Chesterfield, and a Hume, but whose name would have floated down the stream of time, had not shorthand rescued a portion of his labors from oblivion. With so many vouchers for the truth of the remark, we can have no hesitation in stating it as our opinion, that since the invention of printing, no cause has contributed more to the diffusion of knowledge, and the progress of refinement, we might also add, to the triumphs of liberty and the interests of religion, than the revival and improvement of this long-neglected art.

"Such are the blessings which shorthand, like a generous benefactor, bestows indiscriminately on the world at large. But it has additional and peculiar favors in store for those who are so far convinced of its utility as personally to engage in its pursuit. The advantages resulting from the exercise of this art, are not, as is the case with many others, confined to a particular class of society; for though it may seem more immediately calculated for those whose business it is to record the eloquence of public men, and the proceedings of popular assemblies; yet it offers its assistance to persons of every rank and station in life—to the man of business as well as the man of science—for the purpose of private convenience as well as of general information."

A SKETCH OF THE HISTORY OF SHORTHAND.*

An ancient author informs us, that the earliest swift writers proceeded as follows:—Several writers arranged to divide, by signals, or otherwise, a speech or oration into portions of about six or eight words each ; to write these portions in succession, and afterwards compare notes to produce a verbatim transcription of the whole discourse !

The earliest system of ancient shorthand which has been handed down to us, is generally attributed to Cicero ; was practised by Tyro sixty years B.C., and considerably enlarged and expanded by Seneca in the first century. The forms of some of the letters bear a rude resemblance to the Roman and Grecian, and being ill adapted for joining, comparatively few words are written in full, the initial or leading letters being generally used. Plutarch informs us, that the oration of Cato relative to the Catalinian conspiracy, was taken in that system. In his life of Cato, the Younger, he remarks :—" This, it is said, is the only oration of Cato's that is extant. Cicero had selected a number of the swiftest writers, whom he had taught the art of abbreviating words by characters, and had placed them in the different parts of the Senate-house. Before his consulate, they had no shorthand writers."

Shortly after this time, stenography was highly valued among the Romans, and practised even by the emperors. Owing probably to the perishable nature of the writing materials of the Romans (often tablets covered with a layer of soft wax), little is now known either of their systems of shorthand, or of many of the noble, spirit-stirring orations reported therein. From the decline of the Roman empire, in the 5th century, to the reign of Elizabeth, in the 16th century, shorthand was almost unnoticed.

---

* For more complete information, *vide* Lewis's " *Historical Account of Shorthand,*" the *Phonotypic Journal* for 1847, and " Levy's (lately published) " *History of Shorthand.*"

Since the commencement of the 17th century, however, upwards of 200 systems have been published in England !

In 1588, Timothy Bright published, under the the title of " *Characterie*," an attempt at shorthand writing, dedicated to Queen Elizabeth. This was not a system based upon the spelling of words, but consisted of arbitrary characters, each representing a word. Two years later, Peter Bales issued " *The Writing Schoolmaster ;*" and shortly afterwards, an improvement thereon, entitled, "*A New Year's Gift for England.*" Both these works were based on Bright's arbitrary principle.

The credit of inventing a system of English shorthand, based upon spelling, is due to JOHN WILLIS, who, in 1602, published a work, entitled, "*The Art of Stenographie, or Short Writing by Spelling Characterie, invented by John Willis, Batchelor in Divinitie.*" For some of the letters, Willis employed signs requiring two inflections of the pen ; and for Z, a three-stroke sign, " Z." With such an alphabet, the system was, of necessity, slow, tedious, and inefficient. Strange to say, this blunder of judgment was followed by at least sixteen succeeding authors, up to the appearance of Macaulay's "*Polygraphy*" in 1747! This gentleman not only swept away from his alphabet the double-stroke signs, but was the first to *publish* a system containing the sloping curved signs obtainable by dividing a circle into fourths by a perpendicular and horizontal line. Possibly, Macaulay derived his idea of sloping curves from Byrom's alphabet, which, though unpublished, was completed in 1720.

Of the sixteen systems above mentioned, that by Rich (1654) is remarkable for the number of its arbitrary and hieroglyphical characters (upwards of 300), and the absurdity and uselessness of the bulk of them. Speaking of hieroglyphical arbitraries, Mr. Moat, in his "*Stenographic Standard,*" p. 30, styles Mr. Rich "the father of these mysteries ;" and fixing upon three symbols representing respectively, " The devils fear and tremble; the eyes of our understanding are darkened; both houses of parliament ; " Mr. Moat observes that they might with equal propriety be styled, " The devil upon two sticks ; the face of a cat; and two ducks under an arch ! " In a more modern system now before us, a common " *s* " represents a phrase of eighteen words, viz., " Several other remarks might have been made, but as we hasten to a conclusion we shall only state." " *S* " might, with almost equal propriety, stand for a whole sermon! The book of Psalms and the New Testament were engraved and printed in Rich's system.

The two following authors merit special notice:—Farthing (1654), for introducing a small circle for S; and MASON (1682,) for the idea of using *two* forms for S, a small circle, and a stroke sign, and for effecting in other respects considerable improvements upon the alphabets of his predecessors. He was, in fact, the greatest shorthand author of the seventeenth century; Rich being next in order.

In 1751, Thomas Gurney brought out an edition of Mason's system, "*Brachygraphy, by Thomas Gurney,*" the alphabet differing from Mason's in the representation of *i* and *y* only!

In 1748 appeared the first system based on the principle of similar signs for similar articulations, by Jeake. This notion, carried to a ridiculous extreme, coupled with a non-observance of vowels, yielded, as a matter of course, a worthless system. Only imagine *g, j, k, q,* all represented by the same sign, unvaried by length or thickness! The following sets of letters are similarly treated:—*l, r; m, n; b, p, f.*

The above was followed, in 1750, by the first phonetic system, by TIFFIN, which, though objectionable in several features, is decidedly superior to Jeake's rude attempt. Considering the date of his work, Tiffin makes very creditable provision to represent the vowels, throwing the "*a, e, i, o, u,* and sometimes *w* and *y*" basis aside. In fact, a reference to his details, for the purpose of writing out this brief historical sketch, rather surprised us, and very forcibly suggested the thought that the saying of Solomon, that "there is no new thing under the sun," is peculiarly applicable to stenographic matters. We were somewhat astonished to find, in Tiffin's system, the germ of an idea, which, after surmounting many difficulties, we had fully worked out and developed in our own—viz., the writing of diphthongs, or compound vowels, by the junction of the signs representing their component elements. Thus Tiffin represents *oi* by joining *aw* and *ee; ou* by *ĕ* and *oo,*[*] and *ū* by the union of *ee* and *oo.* Here,

---

[*] This analysis of *ou*, if correct, would imply that the present provincial pronunciation of this dipthong (*ĕoo*) in many country places in Lancashire, was, a century ago, prevalent.

however, he stopped, and considering that upwards of a century has since elapsed, it seems a wonder to us that the system we have here developed, should be the first in which the principle is thoroughly and practically applied to the representation of diphthongal vowels generally, whether English, provincial English, or Foreign. Tiffin having selected a sign for *oo* requiring two inflections of the pen, his diphthongs containing this sound (*ou, ŭ*) require three, and are, consequently, too cumbersome and lengthy. His signs for the diphthongs *i* and *oi* are, however, good and practical, viz., V and <. Tiffin was the first to use a small dot for the aspirate.

In 1760 Taplin brought out a system in which he selects similar signs for the similar sounds *k g*, *f v*, *p b*, *t d*, *s z*. He uses perpendicular lines for *t d*; horizontals for *k g*, and a small circle for *s z*. He also hooks straight letters on the left-hand side to add *r*, and on the right to add *l*, with this difference, however, from Mr. Pitman's Phonography; in the former, the hook is joined to the *end* of the consonant; in the latter, to the beginning.

In 1762 appeared Lyle's phonetic system. His analysis of the sounds of language displays considerable phonetic knowledge. He held very clear and correct views as to what a system of shorthand *should be;* unfortunately, however, his disposal of steno-graphic material is strikingly at variance with his theoretical ideas and intentions. He could see what was desirable, but not the method of its attainment.

Another system of phonic shorthand, issued in 1766 by W. Holdsworth and W. Aldridge, of the Bank of England, is, like the above mentioned, impracticable as regards easy writing, but is noteworthy for the circumstance that the authors ground their system on exactly the same analysis of spoken sounds as that which is adopted in the following more recent systems of phonetic writing, viz.:—Row's lengthy, script-like system, 1802 ; George Edmonds's " *Philosophic Alphabet,*" for phonetic longhand and printing, 1832; Isaac Pitman's Shorthand, 1837, &c.

Of the many systems (chiefly unphonetic) which have appeared during the last century, our space will only allow us to notice briefly the most popular or peculiar. Amongst these, that con-structed by DR. JOHN BYROM, of Manchester, in 1720, and pub-lished in 1767, after his death, claims notice. This author bestowed great care in the arrangement of his alphabet, to secure good

joinings and lineality of writing. To effect his object he employed
two signs struck in different directions for eight of his letters, and
three distinct signs for the letter L. His alphabet contains
fourteen signs, commencing with an initial circle. The frequent
requirement of a circle and a stroke to represent *one* letter, greatly
retards the progress of the pen ; and hence, while pleasing to the
eye, Byrom's system lacks the very important requisite of rapidity.
In Molineux's (1823) edition of Byrom, the principle of thickening
a stroke to distinguish the spoken from the whispered letter is
applied to distinguish *v* from *f*, and *z* from *s*. The same thing
occurs in Harding's 5th edition of Taylor's, 1826.

MAVOR, 1780.*—Previous to the introduction of this system,
Shorthand was comparatively little used for reporting public
proceedings. Mason's, Gurney's edition of Mason's, and Byrom's,
were not considered sufficiently brief to repay the trouble of
acquirement, and contracted long-hand was employed by many in
preference. Dr. Johnson reported parliamentary debates in longhand, and boasted that he took care that the Whigs should not
have the best of the argument,—a thing which he could well
manage,—for, instead of *reporting* speeches, he *composed* them, and
that too in the same pompous and grammatical style in which he
himself was accustomed to speak.

A comma, in three positions, is used to represent a, e, i, and a
dot for o, u, y. A comma is objectionable for rapid writing, and
if used at all, should be appropriated to something unimportant,
and of rare occurrence. Mavor's system, although it has gone
through many editions, and has been much practised, is considered
inferior in importance to Taylor's, which followed.

TAYLOR's, 1786.—This, the chief system of the 17th century, is
less perplexing and more simple in its construction than Byrom's,
and is capable of being written with greater speed. This and
Dr. Mavor's system, have done much to forward the art of
shorthand writing in England. Taylor expresses all the vowels
by one dot in any position, thus leading to ambiguity in reading.

In 1823, William Harding, a bookseller, published an improved
edition of Taylor's, in which a light dot, placed before the letter
t, at the beginning, middle, and end, represented respectively

---

* Mavor himself gives 1780 as the date when his system first appeared. Some writers on Shorthand assign it a rather later date.

at, et, it, and a small dash at the top and middle, *ot, ut.* Mr. I. Pitman, who formerly practised Harding's edition of Taylor's, has, in his Phonography, improved upon the above, by adding another dash, in the third position, to represent *oŏt,* &c.

Editions of Taylor's system have been published by Macdougal, 1835; Qdell, 1837; and by Templeton, of Manchester, in 1840.

In 1788, an anonymous system appeared, partially phonetic, named "Brachygraphy," in which the whispered and spoken sounds are represented respectively by short and long characters. Had the author exercised more judgment in the appropriation of signs to paired and unpaired letters, a very fair system might possibly have been the result.

LEWIS, 1815.—This is an ordinary a, b, c, system, which we notice because its inventor is the author of a very interesting *"Historical Account of Shorthand."* He is still living in London, where he teaches his system.

During the last hundred years, the bulk of stenographic authors have come to the conclusion, that a perpendicular stroke works best for *t,* and a sloping upstroke for *r.* The horizontal curve forms have generally been appropriated to *m* and *n,* and by some authors a small circle has been employed for *s.* The notice of a few systems, remarkable for *positional* peculiarities, will bring us to the publication of the most generally practised system of the present century, with which we shall compare our own.

Richardson's system (1800) is much more curious than practical, as the reader may judge by the fact that it is written on a three-barred stave, intersected by two lengths of perpendicular lines about one-eighth of an inch apart, and that in a surface of a fourth of an inch square, places or situations are assigned for twenty letters or words. The writing of a stroke or dot the least remove from the point intended, would give a letter or word entirely different from that which should be committed to paper.

In 1801, Blanc, a Frenchman, followed Richardson with a somewhat similar scheme, but equally impracticable, written on a four-barred stave,

Clive issued, in 1810, a system based upon Mavor's. He distinguishes consonants and words by position, and uses one line only. Consonants represented by similar signs, are differenced by writing one letter on the line, the other under: common words are distinguished by three positions; above, on, and under the line. Clive's amplification of Byrom's idea of differencing common words by position is good, but the plan of thus distinguishing consonants (which Tiffin also used) is objectionable, on account of the arbitrary expedients required when such consonants occur in the middle or at the end of words. This inconvenient arrangement has been adopted in some recent systems. Clive's system would have been much improved had he fixed his lowest position half a t's length higher, viz., *through* the line, instead of *under*. The same remark applies to a system constructed by Farr, in 1819, in which initial vowels and common words and phrases are indicated by three positions,—above, through, and under the line. Both Clive and Farr have attached too little importance to the fact that a writer loses much time by certain aerial motions of his pen over the paper, when the upper and lower portions of the field of writing are too distant from each other. Of the two systems just noticed, Farr's is, on the whole, decidedly the best.

For vowelitic distinctions by position, and positional distinctions between common words,

MOAT, 1833, carries the palm. He writes in a stave of four bars, the upper and lower being formed with two fine double lines. *A, e, o* take, respectively, the upper, middle, and lower space, *i* the middle single line, and *u* the bottom double line. Not content with five places in three-tenths of an inch, he subdivides these five, and thus obtains thirteen "situations," each of which, when dotted, represents a common word. Well may the author remark, —"It is to be understood, then, that a dot dropped upon any of these situations, *fully, clearly*, and *positively*, expresses that word as there laid down." The italics are ours. In addition to the above hair-splitting distinctions, there are niceties of formation in the letters of his alphabet which are quite impracticable in ordinary writing. Mr. Moat was sincerely desirous to advance the art of stenography, and it is to be regretted that his judgment was not more strongly influenced by practical considerations in the compilation of his elaborate, in fact, too elaborate, treatise.

Davidson's system, published in 1847, and written on a similar stave, is much more practical, both alphabetically and "positionally." This author contents himself with five positions in the stave, for *a, e, i, o*, and *u*, respectively. According to a calculation made by Mr. I. Pitman, in the Reporter's Magazine, 1848, this system, for brevity, is, to Pitman's Phonography, as 263 strokes to 253. Davidson, and also Moat, indicated added consonants by the thickening, shortening, or lengthening of the alphabetical characters.

We just refer to Gabelsberger's system, published 1831-4, it being the popular system in Germany. We have carefully examined it (an Anglicised edition), and consider it ill adapted for English reporting. Although its author professes to have constructed it to follow the motions of the pen in longhand writing, many of the outlines for English words are extremely inconvenient. L, for example, is represented by a joined dot!

In 1837 Mr. ISAAC PITMAN's phonetic system appeared under the name of "*Stenographic Sound-hand.*" In a subsequent and improved edition, the name was changed to *Phonography.** This system is a decided improvement upon any previously published. The simple vowels are represented by dots and dashes placed at the beginning, middle, or end of the consonant, the signs being written light or heavy, according to the length of the vowel. The ordinary diphthongs, *i, oi,* and *ou,* and those formed by the coalescence of *y* or *w*, with a following simple vowel, are represented by angular and curved signs; but between these signs, and those representing the elementary sounds forming the compounds, there is no relation whatever. In our work (as noticed under Tiffin's system), the signs for compound vowels are formed from, or have a relation to, the characters representing the simple vowels of which the compounds are composed.

In the case of three out of Mr. Pitman's six couplets of vowels, the short and long vowels are unphonetically paired. They are, *ĕ, a(y); i, ee; ŭ, oh.* An unsuccessful attempt was made, in 1844, to effect an improvement in the last-named couplet, but the three-place scale for the simple vowels presents stenographic obstacles to strict phonetic accuracy, which have not yet been surmounted. A three-place vowel scale is objectionable in the case of half-length consonants. Reckoning ordinary letters at

---

* The meaning of this word is thus quaintly given in the title of a work of 144 pages now before us, and published in London, 1701:— "Practical Phonography : or, the new art of rightly spelling and writing words by the sound thereof; and of rightly sounding and reading words by the sight thereof. Applied to the English tongue, by J. Jones, M.D."

one-eighth of an inch in length, (and they are frequently written
shorter,) a writer of Pitman's system has to recognise three
positions or situations for vowels, by the side of a stroke one
sixteenth of an inch in length. Under such circumstances, the
intended vowel must necessarily often be read by guess from the
context, or the consonantal outline, rather than by a certain and
correct representation. A few years ago, Mr. Pitman considered
two places for an angular vowel as too uncertain for the reader,
and accordingly made a change in the representation of *oi*, and
since then, his angular vowels have had the full scope of the
consonant.

In this new system we have eight simple vowels which may be
pronounced long or short. The pairing of the long and short
sounds is, however, so strictly phonetic, that frequently the writer
need pay little, if any, attention to the thickness of the sign. The
phonetic pairing of the long and short sounds of seven couples out
of the eight, is indisputable, and the pairing of the other couple,
ay, i, if not strictly phonetic, is, in our opinion, a nearer approach
to phonic accuracy than any previous arrangement. The following
remarks on *i* as the short sound of *ay*, formed part of a letter
which we addressed to the editor of the *Phonetic Journal*, and
which was inserted in the number for October 12th, 1861.

"If we cut short the vowel in the second syllable of 'Finlayson,'
the result is, to my mind, not *ĕ*, but *ĭ*; the vowel in the
second syllable being (when shortened) precisely the same as that
in the first. When the vowel in the last syllable of mount*ain*,
cert*ain*, bond*age*, Sund*ay*, Mond*ay*, &c., is shortened by rapid
enunciation, I apprehend that we get mount*in*, cert*in*, bond*ige*,
Sund*y*, Mond*y*, &c., or, at all events, I think that the short sound
of the *ay* is nearer *i* than *ĕ*.

"Most of the readers of the Journal are doubtless aware that
ee i are not considered by phoneticians as a true pair. If then *ee*
is *not* the long sound of *i*, what is? I think *ay*."

We may further remark, that if *ay* is not the long sound of *i*,
this short vowel has no corresponding long sound in English, and
should be considered as an unmodifiable, independent vowel
sound.

By an extension of the principle of distinguishing letters by
thickness of stroke, Mr. Pitman's consonant signs are more simple
and practical than in any previous system. Between the light

and heavy methods of writing some characters, there is, however, no phonetic affinity or relationship, viz. :—curve R and W; L and Y. One of the alphabetical characters has two meanings, phonetically distinct from each other ; CH when the sign is written downwards, and R when written upwards. This arrangement is a source of much trouble to learners, who, though taught otherwise, will in their early practice frequently confound ch and r with each other. In our alphabet, as compared with Mr. Pitman's, there is not only a stronger relation between signs and sounds in the vowel marks, but also in the consonant signs. W, we have paired with WH (HW), preferring, however, for practical reasons, to give the light sign to the sonant rather than to the whispered letter. Y being a modification of the vowel ee, its full-length consonant sign is a lengthening of the ee vowel mark. With Y we have paired H, h having a closer relation to y than to any other consonant. We have represented R by a sloping stroke, written upwards or downwards; a decided advantage both to learner and proficient. The thick downstroke, corresponding to R, is given to its fellow liquid L. When written upwards, the sign for L is differenced from R by extra length instead of thickness ; for though a thick upstroke may be written with a pencil, it is not convenient in pen-written shorthand.

In Pitman's phonography, sh, r, and l, and in ours, w, n, r, l, s, k, and *French nasality*, are represented by signs which can be written downwards or upwards: with the exception of Pitman's downward r, and our downward k, *all these signs slope in the direction of ordinary longhand writing.* The advantages arising from a downward and upward direction for six frequently occurring English letters, and a very common French sound, are manifestly great. We may note that our upward W commences like the vowel oo, of which vowel sound the W coalescent is a modification.

In Pitman's system, an initial hook on the left-hand side of straight letters adds r; and a similar hook on the right-hand side adds l. As the generality of curves will admit, with convenience to the writer and certainty to the reader, of a hook on the concave side only, the application of the above idea to the curve-signs has given rise to irregularities which greatly embarrass and confuse the learner. The r hook is prefixed to the curve R to represent fr, while vr is written by prefixing the r hook to W. *Thr* thr are, in like manner, formed by an initial hook to S Z ; mp is hooked for mr, and ng with initial hook becomes nr.

[A short time after the proposal of the "New word-position scale," noticed in the preface, we wrote Mr. Pitman, remarking, that if he were determined to make alterations, instead of the partial and unsatisfactory changes then proposed, it would be far better to consider the practicability of removing by one sweep, rather than by frequent annoying alterations, certain acknowledged inconsistencies from the system, and to leave the 10th edition undisturbed until a real improvement thereon had been fully matured and tested. We arranged a scheme to remove the inconsistencies which we have just noticed in the curved letters, by bringing them under a general rule to add *r* by an initial hook, *l* by a larger initial hook, and to represent alphabetical R by the same straight line written upwards or downwards, &c., &c. Feeling convinced that changes of this character would, ultimately, be made by Mr. Pitman, we thought it would be well at once to adopt in our own practice what appeared to us as improvements, in order to avoid future inconvenience arising from frequent and partially developed changes. Subsequently, when Mr. Pitman seemed determined to adopt the obnoxious "New word-position scale," we resolved to begin *de novo*, and to construct an entirely new system embodying our ideas, so that we could publish the result of our labours, if we felt disposed.]

We have just noticed Mr. Pitman's arrangements for adding *r* and *l* to the alphabetical characters. We add *r* by an initial hook to any letter of the alphabet, in the case of which, *r* added by a hook will yield an advantage. A large initial hook, or the lengthening of a letter, adds *l*. After providing an *r* hook for all letters which require it, we have a number of spare hooked characters available for other purposes, and have appropriated them for the representation of *w*, *wh*, *wl*, *wd*, *wr*, *wl*, *kw* (= q), upward *k*, and various foreign sounds.

In Pitman's phonography, a small circle has several meanings, according to the side of the stroke to which it is joined: in this system its meaning is the same on either side of straight letters. This gives a great advantage to the writer. Any experienced phonographist is aware, that when a consonant, which should be straight, is written with an initial and final hook or circle, and both on the same side of the stroke, such stroke is apt to take a curved form, to the detriment of the reader. The writing of the circle *s* on either side of a straight line, owing to its tendency to preserve the straightness of the phonograph, gives the writer much more freedom of hand. When one side is as convenient as the other, by writing the circle on the side of the consonant where a vowel should read, such vowel may be *indicated* when not actually written, to the gain of both writer and reader. The above remarks also apply to the large *st* circle. We may here remark, that we have chosen a large circle for *st* rather than *ss*, because the former occurs much oftener than the latter, and the large circle being well adapted for joining, it can be conveniently followed by *r* for the syllable *ster*.

As a general rule, Mr. Pitman adds *n* by a final hook, and *t* or *d* by shortening a letter. Our plan is the reverse. Mr. Pitman lengthens curves to add *tr*, *dr*, or *thr*; we add these syllables by a large final hook, and, as before mentioned, lengthen the signs to add *l*.

Owing to Mr. Pitman's arrangement for adding *t d*, *n*, *tr dr thr*, his rules for reading final appendages to shortened and lengthened letters are open to objection. They greatly perplex the learner, and occasionally produce a momentary confusion in the minds of the very best writers of his system.

In the case of ordinary length letters, final hooks and final circles and loops, follow the same rule; but shortened and lengthened signs follow one rule for final circles and loops, but another, and altogether different rule, for final hooks; and the final hook, though written last, is not read last. The system presented in this little volume is free from this serious defect. The power added by shortening or lengthening, reads before ANY final appendage, and thus whatever is final to the hand and the eye, is final to the reader.

Take for example the letter F in Mr. Pitman's system:—the affixing of a final circle gives *fs*, a final hook *fn*. Thus far the arrangement is orderly; but if the signs be reduced in length, the *t* added by shortening reads *before* the appended circle, but *after* the appended hook. We consider it a more orderly arrangement, that the power added by shortening (or lengthening) should, in *all* cases, read after the primary letter, and before final hooks, circles, or loops, without any exception. One inconsistency often leads to another, and one of the results of Mr. Pitman's scheme for reading final appendages to shortened letters is, the adoption of the anomaly of differencing *d* from *t* by thickening a final N hook!

We have avoided this inconsistency by the simple, straightforward arrangement, that a final hook should follow the same rule as a final circle, and, being written last, should read last.

Having referred to letters represented in Mr. Pitman's system, and in our own, by two forms, or directions, we may remark that the variety of consonantal expression thus obtainable, enables us to difference words containing the same consonants, according to the relation of vowels to the outline, or some other peculiarity. This distinguishing of similar words by their skeleton forms, affords much aid to writer and reader, and may be more fully carried out in this new system than in any previously published.

ETYMOGRAPHY.—Under this title, a very fair system of phonetic shorthand was published in 1842, by Mr. S. A. Good. This gentleman and Mr. I. Pitman were teachers in the same school at Wotton-under-Edge, Gloucestershire, and both worked hard at the construction of a practical system of Phono-Stenography. In some important details (method of hooking to add *r* and *l*, for example) they coincided in opinion; in others, they differed, and published separate works. We think Mr. Pitman exercised a much sounder judgment than Mr. Good, in the choice of consonant signs; but, of the two, we prefer Mr. Good's vowel-scale, which was adopted by Mr. Pitman in his 10th edition, in January, 1858. It is a matter of regret that the superiority of Mr. Good's arrangement was not appreciated earlier; much inconvenience and confusion would, thereby, have been avoided. Mr. Good died a few years ago.

We had prepared notices of several other systems of recent date, but the space at our disposal will not admit of their insertion without detriment to other portions of this work ; we must, therefore, bring our " sketch " to a close.

DEFINITIONS.

PHONETICS, PHONICS, PHONOLOGY (from φωνή, *phōnē*, voice), the science of the human voice, which treats of different elementary sounds and their modifications.

PHONETIC, PHONIC, pertaining to sound; executed phonetically, as phonetic spelling, writing, or printing.

PHONETICIAN, PHONOLOGIST, one skilled in phonetics.

PHONOGRAPHY, (from *phōnē*, voice, and γραφη, *graphē*, writing,) the art of representing spoken sounds, each by its distinctive sign, or character; also the style of writing in accordance with this art.

PHONOGRAPHER, a writer of phonography.

PHONOGRAPHIST, one who not only writes phonography, but is also thoroughly versed in the phonetic and stenographic principles upon which the art is based.

PHONOGRAPH (*noun*), a graphic or written sign representing a certain sound. A phonograph may be simple or compound; it is simple when indicating an elementary sound; compound, when, by a difference in length, an initial or final appendage, or by a combination of these abbreviating principles, the sound represented consists of more than one·vocal element.

PHONOGRAPH (*verb*), to write with phonographs.

When a number of phonographs are joined together so as to form a word, such combination of signs (before the vowels are inserted) is termed an OUTLINE, or SKELETON. A phonograph is sometimes called a *Single Stroke Outline.*

PHONOLOGUE (from *phonē*, voice, and λογος, *logos*, word), a complete phonographic representation of a word, including both outline and vowel, or vowels.

PHONOTYPY, the art of printing in which each sound is represented by a distinct letter, or type; also, the style of printing thus executed.

PHONOTYPE, or PHONOGRAM (from γραμμα, *gramma*, letter), a printed letter or sign indicating a certain spoken sound.

PHONOTYPE (*verb*), to print with phonotypes.

PHRASEOGRAM, a phrase which may be conveniently expressed by joining the outlines of the words of which it is composed. This word is used after the manner of "*Telegram.*"

PHRASEOGRAPH, the joined outlines representing a phrase. A phraseograph is sometimes designated, a phrascographic outline.

PHRASEOGRAPHY, the art or practice of writing phrases without lifting the pen. We use PH. as a contraction for this word.

WORD-SIGN, a letter, or phonograph representing a word.

GRAMMALOGUE, a letter-word; a word expressed by a single letter, or phonograph.

LOGOGRAPH, or CONTRACTED OUTLINE, an abbreviation consisting of *more than one* phonograph, used to represent a word which it would be inconvenient to express by its full skeleton form.

CONTRACTED WORD, a word represented by a logograph.

PHONIC SHORTHAND.

HINTS ON COMMENCING THE STUDY OF THE ART.

The system here presented to the reader is, as its name implies, based upon the phonic principle of spelling, rather than the common *a b c* method. To give arguments in proof of the superiority of a phonetic system of spelling for shorthand purposes would be useless, for the advantages of spelling words according to their sounds are admitted by most of the authors of the old systems, *who recommend their readers to spell by sound,* BUT DO NOT PROVIDE THE MEANS.

The rapidity of the pupil's progress in this, or any other phonetic system, will depend materially on the keeping of the phonic idea before him in the commencement of his practice. It is of great importance that he should, from the first, have a clear apprehension of "the nature and powers of letters, and the just method of spelling words"; not, however, an apprehension in accordance with Lindley Murray's ideas of orthographical propriety, but a conception in harmony with phonetic principles. The student should be careful to discriminate between the old names of certain letters, and the real powers of those letters in the phonetic alphabet. To this end, he should call the signs by the names we have given, rather than by those to which he has, in some cases, been accustomed. The words illustrating the sounds, or powers of the signs, should be carefully examined. *Aw, oo, ng, th, sh, ch, g,* should not be called *ay double yoo, double oh, en jee, tee citch, cs aitch, see aitch, jee*; but should be named in accordance with the real powers of the phonographs, as given in the alphabet. A phonograph, in many cases (the above, for instance), does not express the letters placed opposite, but the SOUND represented by those letters. For example,—to ascertain the exact power of "chay," pronounce *chay* slowly and distinctly, and note the mode of producing the sound. The vowel *ay* should then be gradually separated from the *ch*, and finally, being entirely dropped, the separate sound or power of *ch* will be heard. So with the other signs. If the power of a consonant be required, first pronounce it with a final vowel, and gradually drop the vowel; to arrive at the exact sound represented by a vowel mark, first pronounce the vowel with a following consonant, as *at*, *et*, *it*, then cut off the consonant, and the power of the vowel is clearly heard.

It may be of use to the learner to remark, that a phonograph has always the same meaning or power. Thus " | " invariably represents " T," no matter how this sound may be denoted in the common orthography ; whether by *bt* as in debt, *cht* in yacht, *ct* in indict, *ed* in talked, *ght* in sought, *tt* in Pitt, *phth* in phthisic, or *pt* in receipt, ptyalism, &c. However variable the powers of letters may be in our common spelling, in this system of short-hand they have always the same value. The sounds represented by *ee*, *ay*, *ĭ*, *ĕ*, *oh*, are each represented in the ordinary orthography (incredible as it may appear) by upwards of thirty different methods of spelling, but the method of expressing them does not change in Phonic Shorthand.

We have explained these matters thus fully, for the special benefit of those who have no friend acquainted with the art from whom they could obtain a few oral lessons. Although a teacher is desirable, when obtainable, still we shall give such details that an intelligent reader will find no difficulty in mastering the art by means of this "Handbook" alone.

The student will occasionally find it somewhat difficult to determine what are the sounds which are heard in, and which he should write for, certain words, as a given word may be pro-nounced in several ways by different authorities.* A little phonographic practice will, however, lessen or remove these difficulties. To determine the best and most approved method of pronouncing doubtful words, the youthful student will be led to note more closely the orthoepy of competent authorities and good speakers, and thus, while acquiring phonography, his knowledge of pronunciation will be considerably extended and improved.

---

* It being desirable, that writers of the same system should adopt in their phonologues a pronunciation as uniform as possible, by way of standard, we would suggest the conveniently sized "*Economic and Comprehensive English Dictionary*," lately published by Messrs. W. and R. Chambers, Edinburgh and London, in eight 6d. parts, but which may now be had bound. By the use of contracted words, a very large quantity of matter is given in this volume. The first eighty pages are taken up with an introduction containing a vast amount of ortho-graphical and phonetic information in a concise, plain form, which will be found highly useful to many phonographers. The pronunciation is indicated with very good judgment and considerable exactness, by means of phonotypes. The work as a whole reflects great credit on the enterprising publishers, and is a welcome addition to lexicographical literature.

DIRECTIONS FOR PRACTICE.

Ruled paper is best for phonography, or, indeed, for any system of shorthand. Faint red lines (not too full a shade) are better than blue for gas-light reporting, or under any circumstances where the light is insufficient. Some shorthand writers prefer double-line paper for reporting, as having a tendency to preserve a uniform size of writing, and to prevent the formation of too large characters. Much depends on the habits of a writer. Some write small and neatly on single-line; others with clumsy, straggling forms on double-line. Single-line is most economical, and double-line yields no advantage to the practised writer, if the upper line be more than a full tenth of an inch distant from the lower one. Learners may find it advantageous in their early practice to use double-line, but in such cases the lines should be distant from each other one-eighth of an inch. We suggested to Mr. Fred Pitman, 20, Paternoster Row, London, that in double-line paper, the lower, or principal line, should be slightly thicker than the upper; and he informs us that he intends to keep in stock single-line, and close and open double-line reporting paper, in red or blue. Obtainable through the booksellers, in five quire packets, 1s. 6d. Cases for holding paper when reporting, 1s. 3d., morocco, 3s.

A fine-pointed gold pen, or a medium-pointed steel pen, will be found best for shorthand. It is well, however, to write occasionally with a pencil, so as not to be altogether unaccustomed to its use when pen and ink are not procurable. Moseley's patent fountain pens are very convenient for reporting, as they save the necessity for carrying an inkstand about. When an excise bottle is used, it should be carefully selected, many being faulty either in the length of the tube, or its aperture. The aperture at the bottom of the tube should not be too small, or the lower part of the holder will get daubed with ink; and to secure a good dip, there should be about three-quarters of an inch between the bottom of the tube and the bottom of the bottle. That the ink may not escape when the bottle is inverted, the space above the bottom of the tube should exceed that which the ink occupies. However good the bottle, it is well to use a cork when not in use. When writing on the knee, the ink-bottle is generally held in the left hand, the thumb being passed through a loop formed by a piece of tape attached to the neck of the bottle. The bottle may also be hung to a twisted wire, attached to the back or hinge of the reporting cover, by passing the wire through loops, thus leaving the left hand at liberty. We prefer this method.

The student should, in his early practice, write slowly and carefully, and form the characters as though he were drawing rather than writing: practice will give rapidity. If, however, he care more at first to write fast than well, he will probably not only hinder his attainment of true swiftness, but confirm himself in a slovenly and somewhat illegible style of writing. The hand and arm should rest, and the pen or pencil be held as for drawing, or reversely sloped common-hand. In this position d, y, b, &c., can be most easily struck.

Write much, in order to become familiar with the new signs; and to further this object, speak aloud the names of the characters while writing them: the ear, the eye, and the hand are thus trained at the same time. The learner will also find it advantageous to sharpen his pencil at the blank or unleaded end, and with this wooden point to trace the characters as he goes through the reading exercises.

For early writing exercises, short words of one or two syllables are recommended; such, for example, as the easy sentences in books for teaching ordinary reading. Or, taking ordinary matter, the short words may be written, and the long ones omitted. After a few weeks' study and practice (to which at least an hour a day should be given), the student will find himself prepared to include in his exercises the more complicated words; and if he is persevering, and will take care to master one thing before he passes on to another, he will find the acquisition of this system of shorthand a pleasing rather than an irksome labour. It will be well for the beginner to bear in mind that there is no royal road to learning. PERSEVERE! should be the motto of every young phonographer, for PRACTICE, and nothing but PRACTICE, can give and increase facility. Those, therefore, who intend to enjoy the advantages of writing shorthand, must be willing to bestow the necessary labor. It has been said that "he who will have no knowledge, but that for which little exertion has been used, must, one time or other, suffer the mortification of finding what he possesses to be of small intrinsic worth."

PLAN OF LESSONS

TO ACQUIRE A KNOWLEDGE OF THIS SYSTEM IN TWO MONTHS.

The following will be found of service, both to teachers and to the self-taught. It is to be considered simply as a rough draft, to be modified according to circumstances. The lessons may be reduced to SIX, or extended to TWELVE, or upwards; in the latter case, taking up the system more gradually. We prefer to introduce the principles of abbreviation at a moderately early period of tuition, in order that the pupil may accustom himself as little as possible to long outlines for words which, a few weeks later, may be written with much greater ease, clearness, and brevity. The pupil should be required to *unlearn* as few outlines as possible. It is for this reason that we have recommended the student to write short words in his early practice, leaving the longer ones until he has provided himself with the means for their convenient representation.

FIRST WEEK.—The simple vowels, ordinary diphthongs, and the simple consonants, with the manner of using these letters; which includes the general rules for placing and reading vowels.

SECOND WEEK.—Initial *w* hook; double consonants, and the relation of vowels to these compound letters. Also bring into use the Word-signs for about a dozen of the most frequently occurring grammalogues, given first in the general list.

THIRD WEEK.—A few more word-signs. Adding of *tr, dr, thr.* Shortened and lengthened signs with final annexments. Additional representation of *ss*. Use of initial and final loops. If more work be desired, look over the *w, h, y,* and *ee* series of vowel-marks.

FOURTH WEEK.—The vowelitic compound signs just mentioned. Familiarize the mind with preceding lessons, particularly with the writing and reading of vowels. Commit to memory the prefixes and affixes, and acquire further knowledge of the word-signs. Attend to the general rules for writing outlines.

FIFTH WEEK.—Rules for locating word-signs and outlines with respect to the line. Study the list of best outlines for common words, and learn the principal logographs. Review preceding lessons.

SIXTH WEEK.—The representation of diphthongs and foreign sounds. Go through the list for differencing, by variety of outlines, words containing the same consonants. Observe the manner of forming phraseographs. Again note the details of previous lessons.

SEVENTH WEEK.—Give further attention to single-stroke outlines, logographs, and phraseographs; also examine carefully the reading exercises, and re-write them. The adding of *lr.*

EIGHTH WEEK.—Thoroughly re-peruse the whole "Handbook," and in this and following weeks practise as much as possible to acquire familiarity with outlines, and, consequently, SPEED IN WRITING.

VOWELS.

We recognise in the English language eight elementary vowel sounds, which sounds may be varied in length or duration. They are heard—

Short in	Long in
1. *at, am.*	1. *aft, palm.*
2. *ebb, err, per.*	2. *ere, air, pair.*
3. *e-vince, e-lect.*	3. *eve, eel.*
4. *it, ill.*	4. *ate, ail (See page 20).*
5. *on. cot.*	5. *awn, caught.*
6. *up, love.*	6. *urn, word.*
7. *o-mit, o-pine.*	7. *o-men, o-pen.*
8. *pull, foot, could.*	8. *pool, food, two.*

The above simple vowels are represented by dots, dashes, and curves, written light or full, and in two positions, as in Table, page 33. The perpendicular line is the letter T, used to exhibit more clearly which vowels are written to the beginning, and which to the end of a consonant. The beginning of a letter is the portion first written, irrespective of downward or upward direction.

The most commonly used diphthongs are I (as in *by*), OI, OW, and U, = *yoo.*

Dots excepted, the length of a vowel-mark is considered to be one-fourth that of a consonant.

Except in special cases, vowel-signs should not be written so close as to touch the phonograph to which they relate.

The simple dash-vowels are written at a right angle with the consonant; or, if more convenient, with a slight variation from such an angle. Curved and hooked vowel-marks must always be written in the position given in the Table.

The small signs for *I, OW*, are contractions of the longer, full characters, which latter form portion of a series of diphthongs, partly foreign. (See pages 66-7.) The small signs for *I* and *OW* should not be joined to consonants as vowel-marks. When joined, they have the powers of *F* and *T* respectively. *(See Consonants.)*

The *w, h, y,* and *ee* series of compound phonographs, are modifications of the signs for the simple vowels and ordinary diphthongs.

We have inserted here the series of initial *ee dissyllabic* diphthongs, on account of their close relationship in use, power, and written form, to the *y* series.

A dot being, under some circumstances, inconvenient for joining to other small signs, a small hook may be used instead. Such hook should, however, be joined to that side of the preceding, or

following stroke, which will not interfere with joined *curve* vowels.
(*See Table.*) The writer may, by a subsequent touch of the pen,
transform a small hook into a dot, but this is unnecessary.

The following observations will perhaps give the learner a little
mnemonic assistance.

In compound vowel-marks, *oo* may be used for *w*, and *ee* for *y*.

Wah weh, wee way, and their short sounds, are formed by the
junction of the signs for the simples; *waw wuh* and *woh woo* are
represented, respectively, by the initial portion of the downward
and upward *curve W*, which signs resemble, and are suggestive of,
those for *au uh, oh oo*, which follow the *w*.

English "aspiration" being an unusually strong expulsion of
breath when pronouncing a vowel, we have expressed *H* by a
slight addition to, or variation of, the vowel sign :—*hah heh*, by an
additional small dot, the two dots being written parallel with the
consonant; *hee hay*, by an upward tick to the dash vowel; *haw
huh, hoh hoo*, by lengthening, in a horizontal direction, one end of
the simple vowel signs; *hi, hou, hwi*, by thickening the signs for
i, ou, wi.

H may be expressed before a double letter of the *w*, or *y* series,
as shown in the Table.

EE precedes Nos. 1, 2, 3, and 4 vowels, dissyllabically, by
writing the *ee* phonograph perpendicularly. *EE* forms a dissyllabic
diphthong with the curve vowels, by angularising the curves.

The generality of students should not attempt to use the *w*, *h*,
y, and *ee* series of letters in their early practice. After a few weeks,
they can adopt them as they may find convenient. Too many
things at a time will confuse the mind.

Vowels written near the beginning of consonants are called
first-place vowels; those placed near the end, second-place vowels.

To test the phonetic accuracy of the vowel-scale, pronounce the
simple vowels in pairs, and observe the very slight modification of
the organs of speech in passing from the short to the long, or the
long to the short. There is also an approximation in character
between the power expressed by a given vowel-mark when written
at the beginning of a phonograph, and its power when written at
the end. In proof, pronounce a first-place vowel and a second-place
vowel represented by the same sign, and note the very slight
variation or disturbance of the vocal organs in changing from the
one to the other.

Although greater facilities are afforded in this system than in
any previously published, for the exact expression of vowels, yet,
owing to the full extent to which the principle of "similar signs
for similar sounds" is carried, an accidental lack of precision on
the part of the writer, will be less likely to give the reader inconvenience in this scheme, than in other professedly phonetic
systems.

Simple Vowels;—
heard SHORT and LONG in the words given.

SHORT. LONG.			SHORT. LONG.	
1 ă	AH	ălărm Àhā!	5 ŏ	AW ŏnslaught
2 ĕ	EH	{ĕnsnāre, everywhēre}	6 ŭ	UH ŭnfürl ŭnwŏrthy
3 eĕ	EE	rĕvēal, rĕprieve	7 oh	OH prŏpōse
4 ĭ	AY	Ĭsrāel inlāy	8 oŏ	OO fŏŏt-stoŏl full-mōōn

COMMON DIPHTHONGS.

I, as in "ice". | OI as in "oil". | OW as in "owl".
or for joining, and pronoun I. eyes, Isaac | Ū = YOO.

Signs for Vowels preceded by—
W.(oo) H. Y.(ee) EE (dissyllabic.)

		W.(oo)		H.		Y.(ee)		EE (dissyllabic.)	
1	ă · AH	wă · WAH	hă · HAH	yă · YAH		
2	ĕ · EH	wĕ · WEH	hĕh · HEH	yĕh · YEH	ee-ă	ee-ĕh
3	eĕ · EE	weĕ · WEE	heĕ · HEE	yeĕ · YEE		
4	ĭ · AY	wĭ · WAY	hĭ · HAY	yĭ · YAY	ee-ĭ	ee-ay
5	ŏ · AW	wo · WAW	hŏ · HAW	yŏ · YAW	ee-ŏ · EE-AW
6	ŭ · UH	wŭ · WUH	hŭ · HUH	yŭ · YUH	ee-ŭ · EE-UH
7	oh · OH	woh · WOH	hoh · HOH	yoh · YOH	ee-oh · EE-OH
8	oŏ · OO	woo · WOO	hoŏ · HOO	yoo · YOO	ee-oo · EE-OO / EE-YOO
	I	WI	HI or	YI written upward	EE-I
	OI	WOI	HOI	YOI	EE-OI
	OW	WOW	HOW	YOW	EE-OW

"H" preceding the "W Series".

"H" preceding the "Y Series".

The full-sized, consonantal representation of
H, HW, HY is sometimes more convenient than the
small compound letters. See next page.

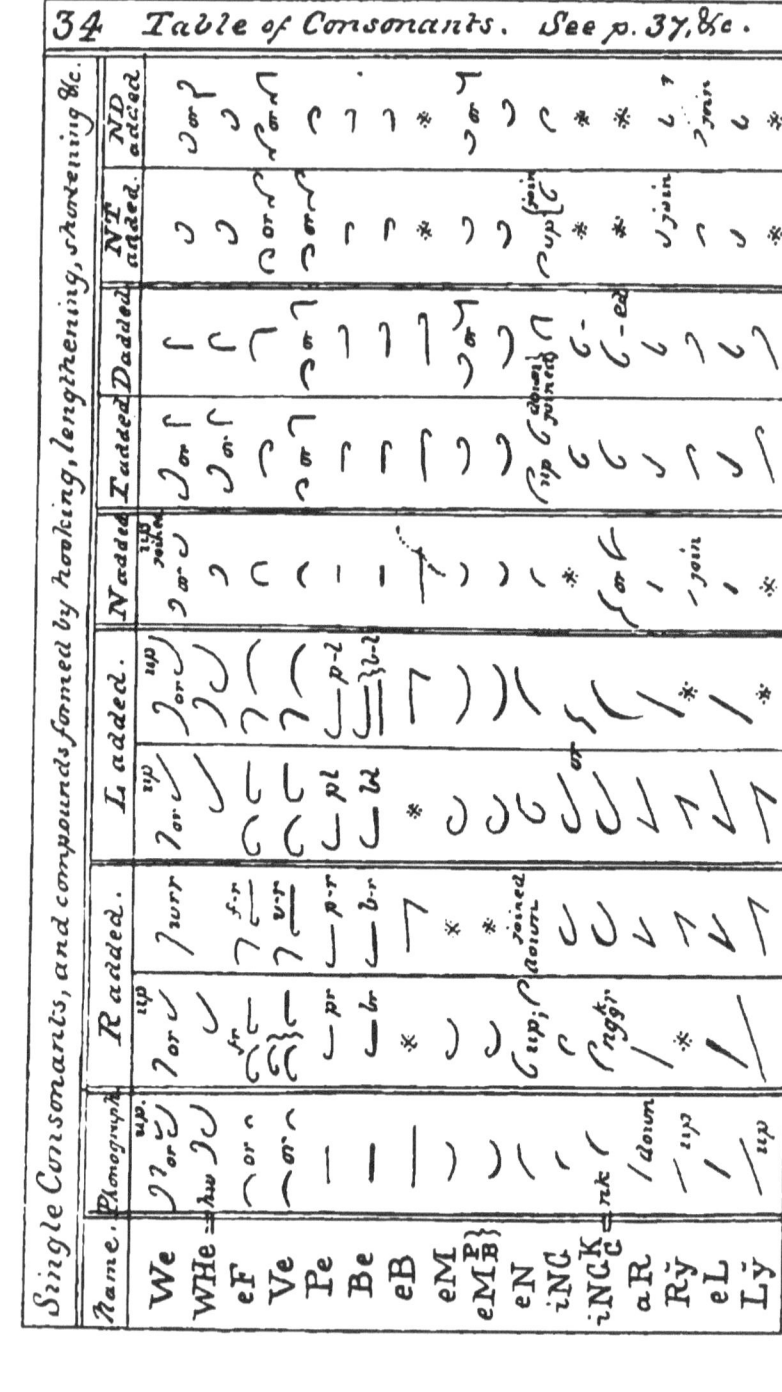

Single Consonants, and compounds formed by hooking, lengthening, shortening &c.

| eS |
| eZ |
| eTH |
| THe |
| Te |
| De |
| CHay = tsh |
| Jay = dzh |
| iSH |
| iZH |
| Kay |
| Gay |
| eK |
| KWé = Q |
| Haitch |
| Ye |
| HYoo |
| LETTERS JOINED. |

Phonologues illustrating rules for writing initial, medial and final vowels. P 37-8

away await aft eve or event about open opened opinion aim ample imi-[nel] impose own unsafe ink air ail welfare easy head ahead each edge or wishes ache egg accordance or eagle hug offer afraid over apply honourable[quaint] authorised idleness accrue acquit ac- week wicked or whip waves ma-son suppose supper cities setter detailed take attack or state sit stay ask us sack seem assume stablish establish why whine or while or white one when fee foot free find or Phonography or vote frequent pay pays pain pains paint pained profanity know noon not meek much ray relinquish readiness reverend luckily life saw assigned assault choice Manchester justice justify during distant displeasure defensive di- vidend or devote wait widow whiten shouldst show call cool sickly school Christian class disgrace accountable contend Queen or example expensive extemporized correct clerical hamper or historical humorist yesterday used hue or suit summer simper sacred descriptive Dec. first virtue personal perversity opportunity important or mercy dear sure shorthand arrange calculate her tenure

* The advanced writer need not intersect s-r p-r v-r b-r & kr.

REMARKS ON THE TABLE OF CONSONANTS; RULES FOR PLACING AND READING VOWELS, &c.

Before going fully into details, it may be well to remark that this system may be practised in various degrees of brevity. In proportion to the extent to which the principles of abbreviation, word-signs, phraseographs, &c., are adopted, we have,—the elementary, or Learners' Style; the medium, or Correspondence Style; and the advanced, condensed, or Reporters' Style.

In his early practice, the pupil need not use the small forms for *f, v, t, d,* and the thin *eb,* but may adopt them at pleasure. The thin forms for *v* and *b* are provided to lessen the necessity for writing *thick* horizontal signs. *EB* is nearly a double length sign; *PP* nearly treble length.

We commenced the vowel-scale with the gutturals, or throat letters, and ended with the labials, or those formed by the lips: the list of consonants commences with the labials, and ends with the gutturals. The labials take the horizontal signs, except *W*, *WH*, which are classed with the liquids inclined in the direction of common writing. The perpendicular signs are appropriated to the dentals, or teeth letters, and the downward left to right signs, to the post-palatals and gutturals. The reader will observe that many of the letters go in pairs, a thin sign generally representing a light, sharp, or whispered letter; a thick sign the corresponding heavy, flat, or spoken articulation.

The signs are to be struck in the most convenient direction,— generally, from top to bottom, or, in the case of horizontals, from left to right. *N* is always written upwards when standing alone, and stroke *S* downwards: when joined to other strokes, these letters may be written upwards or downwards according to con- venience in joining, &c. Downward *N*, upward *S*, and upward curve *W* are only used when preceded or followed by another stroke. An attached hook, circle, or loop is *not* reckoned a stroke. The small forms for *W* are generally joined, except when used for word-signs. Hooked *eK* is always written upwards. An un-joined *upward* straight line, with or without hook, circle, or loop, should slope thirty degrees from the horizontal; when struck downwards, sixty degrees. Circle *S* or *ST* occurring between two phono- graphs, should be written with the most direct, short, and conve- nient motion, or that which best preserves the contour or form of the characters. A circle is generally written inside a curve, except in such combinations as *msn,* in which the circle takes the convex side of one curve (*m*), and the concave side of the other (*n*). The strokes *S, Z* are to be used for words commencing with a vowel followed by *S* or *Z*; or for words ending with a vowel preceded by

S or *Z.* This arrangement includes words in which *S* or *Z* is the only stroke consonant. Full-sized *F*, *T*, and *D* follow the rule just given for *S*, *Z.* The long *V* and *B* should generally be used for words commencing with a vowel followed by *V* or *B*; or for dissyllabic words ending with a vowel preceded by *V* or *B.* Alphabetical *N* is required when a word ends with a vowel preceded by *N*, unless the vowel be *joined* to a half length letter.

When an outline is two or more strokes in depth, the bottom of the first generally rests on the line, the others follow. In writing a word, the consonant outline, or skeleton, is first formed without lifting the pen, and the vowels are afterwards inserted according to the following

RULES FOR PLACING AND READING VOWELS.

A vowel written *above* a horizontal letter, or on the *left* hand side of any other letter, reads BEFORE the consonant.

A vowel written *below* a horizontal letter, or on the *right* hand side of any other, reads AFTER the consonant.

In the case of double consonants, with initial *r*, or *l*-hook, a preceding vowel reads before the *first* letter of the double consonant; a vowel placed after the phonograph, follows the *last* letter, viz., the added *r* or *l.*

The *r* and *l*-hook signs excepted, vowels placed to a phonograph have always reference to the full-length *primary stem, and are uninfluenced by initial or final appendages, or by shortening:* initial circle *s*, *st*, hook *w*, and small signs for *f*, *v*, *t*, *d* must therefore read *first,* and any final appendage *last,* the vowel or vowels having reference to the original stem just as if no initial or final letter was appended. *N* added by halving, follows the same rule as a final hook, or circle. Careful attention to the above remarks will save the learner much trouble. (For examples, see page 36.)

Vowels BETWEEN *consonants:*—When a vowel occurs *between* two *stroke* consonants, if a *first-place* vowel, write it AFTER THE FIRST consonant; if a *second-place* vowel, BEFORE THE SECOND consonant.

Lengthened characters are vocalized in accordance with this rule, the *last half* of the sign being considered as the added *l, r,* or *lr.*

The above general rule does not apply when the first of two strokes is halved for *n*, or when two strokes are separated by the circle *s;* added *n* being the *second* letter in the former case, and circle *s* in the latter.

Vowels may be read *between* the two letters composing the *r* and *l*-hook double consonants, by striking the required vowel through the phonograph when a convenient angle is presented. When otherwise, intersect the double consonant in the *middle* by a small dash, and write the vowel sign after the phonograph. The character being divided by the intersecting dash, into two halves, a first-place vowel may take the whole range of the first half, and a second-place vowel the other half; the vowel may, therefore, be written close by the dash, instead of at the end of the phonograph.

As the lengthened uncurved signs for *f-r, f-l, v-r, v-l,* and *p-r, p-l, v-r, v-l, imply* a vowel between the two letters of the compound phonograph, the intersection of these signs may be disregarded, as remarked on page 36.

When preceded by *T, D,* downward *R, L,* &c., the initial hook of the *curves* appropriated to *fr, fl, vr, rl,* cannot be written without lifting the pen This inconvenience is avoided in *this* system, and also additional facilities secured for joining to *following* characters, by giving the practitioner the option of writing the stem curved or *straight.* This arrangement also enables us to distinguish between words, without writing the vowels, as in the case of the verbs to "*free*," and to "*offer*;" the straight form being used for the latter.

The signs with initial *r* or *l*-hooks may, for the most part, be regarded as diphthongal consonants;* signs *lengthened* to add *L,* are, generally speaking, not diphthongal. Phonographs, in which a large initial hook takes the form and *direction* of the small *v,* are not used for the *L* hooked series, the *v* power for the hook being more useful. It so happens, that in the instances referred to, an initial large hook is *not* required for the adding of *L* diphthongally, its use for *v* is, therefore, a clear gain. In the case of phonographs in which a small initial hook is used for *W,* such hook enlarged is *hw* or *wh,* unless written in the direction of *v.*

Lengthened and Shortened Signs.—As a general rule, we add *L* by lengthening. The exceptions are,—*eB, PP, BB*; all lengthened, uncurved horizontals, except "____ *bl*;" lengthened thin straight lines, sloped in the direction of *r,* and the *l*-hook series, lengthened.

The exceptions to the adding of *N* by shortening, are,—small *V* and *NG.* A half length sign is more convenient than a full length for the frequent termination *ing,* and *ngn* is not required in English. Shortened *fn* is distinguished from small *v,* by deepening the curve for *fn.*

MP and *MB* may be distinguished by deepening the curve for the latter. This is seldom necessary.

Final hooks.—Ordinarily, a final hook adds *t* to thin signs, and *d* to thick ones; but in the case of a few common words, *d* may be added to a light sign, and *t* to a heavy one, as in the words, "*mentioned, great,*" &c. To straight lines, *t* takes one side, *d* the other, as in Table, pages 34, 35.

---

* For convenience, we use the term "diphthongal," in relation to consonants, as well as vowels. This class of compounds should be pronounced like *fr, pr, fl, pl,* in the words *free, prey, flee, play,* &c., and not *ef ar, ef el,* &c.

A *large* final hook adds TR, DR, or THER. With straight stems, TR takes the T side, DR, THR, the D side. The THER hook also represents the words *there, their*. A vowel (generally *yoo*,) may be read between *t-r* and *d-r*, by writing it to the convex side of the hook, as in the words given on page 39. THR may follow a final hook, or curve vowel sign, by a second hook or curve, written in the same direction as the first. See opposite page.

When deemed desirable, a *t* hook may be thickened for *d;* a large final hook for *dr*, or *thr;* an *s* circle for *z*, and an *st* circle for *zd*, &c.

SS, SZ, ZZ may be represented, according to convenience, by stroke and circle *s;*—by circle and stroke *s* or *z;*—by a second back *s* circle following the first, on the opposite side of the stem, and by an independent loop, *not* formed in part by any preceding or following stroke. See opposite page.

Loops.—An initial loop, of which the following consonant stem forms the second half, represents *s* preceding the initial hook phonograph. Circle *s* may also be written within an initial hook. The diphthongal combinations *spr, str, skr*, &c., may be distinguished from *s-pr, s-tr, s-kr*, &c., by using the loop for the former, and circle *s* within the hook for the latter. The hyphen indicates a vowel.

S may precede a large initial *l*-hook, either by writing the circle within the hook, or by an initial loop, turned at its commencement, so as to intersect the stem.

A final loop, formed partially by the stem of the preceding consonant, represents a final small hook followed by *s*. For a *large* final hook followed by *s*, write the circle within the hook. See p. 39.

The side on which a vowel is written to read before a phonograph, is named the *fore*-side; the opposite side, the *after*-side.

When circle *s* is joined to a straight consonant, and one side is as convenient for the writer as the other, the circle is written on the fore-side if a vowel precedes the stroke, and on the after-side if a vowel follows. When, in a single stroke outline, one vowel precedes, and another follows the stem, the writing of the circle *s* on the *fore*-side will generally be most useful for the reader.

Best Outlines.—As a general rule, those outlines should be chosen which, while free and facile, also allow the writer to express clearly the required vowels. Outlines should be preferred for short, primitive words, which, by a simple addition thereto, (without alteration of original outline,) may represent the more lengthy derivatives.

Joining Half-Sized Phonographs.—Except in the case of initial small *v*, and a few unmistakeable combinations such as, *knb* can be; *j̇ j mnt*, (or *j mnt*) judgment; *cks pshn* exception; *pr pṙshn* proportion, &c., half sized signs should not be joined when the point of junction is not defined by an angle. Full-sized *p n, t n*, must, therefore, be used in the words, "cheapen, pippin, Ashton," &c.

Hook representation of TR, DR & THER.

Exs:– whether father Peter pander brighter matter mother all their order writer reader shall there literary arbitrary remainder characters. Creator together embitter embittered bitters bitterest feature lecture. but there did there let their under their cannot their to their of their though there

Representation of SS, SZ.

or causes Misses Mrs or places. tresspasses Moses diseased deceased

The SS loop may be vocalized:–

or schism exercises accessory necessary is as much as is the case &c

INITIAL and FINAL LOOPS.

spray sapper sprightly separately split supplicate several such are or stray as true is true or secluded swear as were as we are sweet swell or as well Scripture succour sphere fits notes mates dates deeds contents hands pounds acts goods that is all its "T" follows a loop by a back hook x mightest didst

The "FLer" series of Treble Consonants.

By lengthening a CURVE hooked for L, r is added

floor — flower — simpler — exemplary

clear — declare — or — glory — irregular

TREBLE LENGTH SIGNS. "LR" Added.

fuller — traveller — or smaller

or — similar — or rider — scholar

circular — regular — or tailor — or dealer

PREFIXES.

ACCOM — . or accommodate — accomplish.

CON — or — (kn) } May also be indicated by a light
joined

COM — } initial dot, or by "proximity".

contention — consequence — or — contract. — compound

conscious — complain — or — committee — to decompose

discomfit — disconcert — concomitant — has computed

I have full confidence — in the comparison

CIRCUM — . — circumstantial.

FOR — . [— form] — former — forgive

FORE — x — foremost — forego

IN — joined . interest — inform — independent

INCON^M — disjoined, or — joined . inconvenient — incomplete
inconstant.

R added to L-hook signs.—As the lengthening of these signs to add a *second L,* would give but a very slight advantage, the lengthening of this series, (the uncurved horizontals excepted,) adds the fellow liquid *R.* *R* is also added to downward *R* and upward *K,* by lengthening. In vocalizing, the last half of the sign is considered as the added *R.*

LR added.—Signs which can be lengthened for *L,* (*B* excepted), if written nearly treble length, receive the addition of *LR,* instead of *L.* The last half of these phonographs is considered as the added *LR.* A vowel may be read between the *L* and the *R,* by intersecting the *lr* portion of the phonograph. See page 40.

The use of these treble-length signs is, of course, optional. For reporting, in which free, speedy outlines are important considerations, these signs will be found very serviceable, as three, four, five, or even six consonants may be represented without an angle, by one phonograph.

PREFIXES AND AFFIXES.—SEE PAGES 40, 43.

The principle which most stenographic authors have adopted, in forming contracted prefixes and affixes, is that of *disjoining* a letter, to save the necessity of writing others which follow: by writing such disjoined letter pretty close to the remainder of the word, its character as a prefix or affix is indicated. In accordance with this principle, the frequent syllables *com, con,* may be indicated by using a preceding syllable, word, or phrase, as a prefix, as in the examples given. Word-signs may also be used as prefixes or affixes, in the formation of compound words. To secure greater uniformity in writing habits, we have included in our list of prefixes and affixes, uncontracted, yet brief, joining forms for some initial and final syllables. In rapid writing, *contracted* prefixes and affixes may often be joined without ambiguity, or, in some cases, entirely omitted. Examples:—*In,* joined to *vn nt,* for *inconvenient; ak* joined to *pl sh* in *accomplish,* or *pl sh* only, may be written for this word; *p n* for *accompany; s dr* for *consider; tnt mnt* for *contentment, ps b* for *possibility,* &c. A syllable may precede and be joined to a prefix sign, as *n d* in the word *undecomposed, ms* disjoined, or *ms kn* joined, in *misconduct,* &c.

Affixes.—*ED* may be represented either by the stroke or hook *d* joined to preceding consonant, or by the affix dot: the latter is generally used when *ed* or *d* is preceded by an end hook, circle, or loop. The dot *ed* and tick *ing* should not be used unless *ed, ing,* form distinct, independent syllables. If written horizontally or perpendicularly, the *ing* tick may be joined. When it is inconvenient to join *L* for the termination *ly,* the phonograph may be disjoined like an affix. Disjoined *ly, ing, ed,* may often be omitted in reporting.

Those who think it desirable, may carry out the principle for forming affixes to a greater extent than we have here exhibited. Exs:—Disjoined *bl, -bleness;* disjoined *f, -fullness;* vowel *aw,* written at the end as an affix, for *-ology, -ologist, -ological-ly,* or for *alogy,* &c.

(For remarks on Prefixes and Affixes, see preceding page.)

Substitution of Signs.—The signs for the similar sounds *ch sh, j zh* may occasionally be interchanged to secure a more convenient joining:—thus *sh* instead of *ch* in the phrases, *of which, of such; chn* for *shn (tion); zh* instead of *j* in the word *per-centage,* &c.

Imperfect Hooks.—In some cases, when a hook cannot be perfectly formed, it may be partially expressed by writing the beginning of one stroke so as to fall on, and form part of, the preceding one. Exs:—Upward *r* and *gr;* downward *sr* and straight *rr : int* and upward *r.* as in the word "interpret," top of opposite page.

VOWELS INDICATED BY POSITION OF OUTLINES.

Write ABOVE the line,—The generality of words *commencing* with a *first*-place vowel ; also word-signs and short words with first-place vowel, whether initial or otherwise.

Write ON the line,— Lengthy outlines, *not* commencing with a vowel ; also word-signs and short outlines with *non*-initial second-place vowel.

Write THROUGH the line,—Outlines *commencing* with a *second*-place vowel. Occasionally, horizontals and small signs may be written *under* the line.

Remarks.—With double-line reporting paper, some writers may prefer, in some instances, to subdivide the words of the *first* position, by writing those *commencing* with a vowel *higher* than those with initial consonant.

The diphthongs *i* and *oi* are considered first-place, their component elements being first-place vowels. *OW* and *YOO (U)* are classed with second-place vowels, their final elements belonging to this class. Occasionally, short words containing non-initial *ow, yoo,* are written through the line. The diphthongs *i* and *ow* may be written to any part of a consonant, beginning, middle, or end.

When a word contains several strokes, the first descending stroke, or non-horizontal letter, is written in the specified position. In the case of lengthened phonographs, (non-horizontals) the *first half* is placed in position in accordance with the preceding rules, the last half being regarded as a second stroke. In such words as "spirit, subject," the *sp* and *sb* word-signs are written above the line, on account of the habit of writing the signs in this position for the full outline.

In phrase writing, *the first word, or word-sign, in a phraseograph retains its assigned position, and governs the following words.* With small, or horizontal first-position word-signs, there is, however, scope for a *very slight* accommodation to following words, but initial word-signs resting on the line must *strictly* retain their position.

To avoid clashing with others, a few word-signs do not follow the general rules for location. Exs :—*Came, gave,* written through the line to distinguish from *come, give.*

INTER ⌐ or ⌐ . ⌐ interrupt ⌐ interpret

IRRECON ⌐ , ⌐ or ⌐ . ⌐ or ⌐ irreconcilable

MAGNI ⌐ . ⌐ magnitude ⌐ magnificent

RECON ᴹ / or ⌐ . ⌐ recompence ⌐ reconstruct
(joined) ⌐ recommend ⌐ reconcile

SELF ⌐ . ⌐ or ⌐ selfish, ⌐ or ⌐ self-conceit ⌐ self-love

UN ⌐ or ⌐ joined . ⌐ unprepared ⌐ unintelligent

UNCON ᴹ ⌐ or ⌐ disjoined . ⌐ unconditional ⌐ uncombined

UNL ⌐ or ⌐ . ⌐ or ⌐ unlike . [ENL ⌐ enlist]

UNR ⌐ or ⌐ . ⌐ unrepresented . UNR-L ⌐ .

AFFIXES.

Contracted affixes are generally indicated by disjoining the phonograph which precedes the omitted letters.

ALITY, ARITY. Disjoin preceding phonograph
⌐ formality ⌐ or ⌐ originality ⌐ or ⌐ congeniality
⌐ instrument-ality ⌐ desirability ⌐ universality
⌐ fragility ⌐ infidelity ⌐ partiality ⌐ nationality
⌐ popularity ⌐ disparity ⌐ prosperity ⌐ inferiority

ED or D final dot . ĕ . ⌐ compounded ⌐ . bettered

EVER ⌐ or ⌐ . ⌐ or ⌐ wherever ⌐ whatever.

ING (or i dash . ⌐ or ⌐ having ⌐ writing ⌐ shutting.

INGLY (ngly, or thicken "ing" tick ⌐ accordingly ⌐ boasting

INGTON (disjoined . ⌐ Paddington ⌐ or ⌐ Wellington

-ING A ⌐ having a . -ING HE ⌐ thinking he

-ING THE ⌐ or ⌐ making the ⌐ noting the

SELF join circle S, and omit L or F, or both . ⌐ or ⌐ thyself
⌐ or ⌐ himself ⌐ herself ⌐ yourself ⌐ myself ⌐ it-self.

SHIP ⌐ . ⌐ or ⌐ fellowship ⌐ Lordship ⌐ worship.

SOEVER ⌐ . ⌐ whatsoever ⌐ wheresoever ⌐ whosoever (whom) soever

TION (shn) join half length SH, or ((chn) if better to join

SELVES disjoined o .) o themselves or ⌐ ; ⌐ or ⌐ yourselves

— *CTION* (= *NSHON*) *by intersecting preceding letter*
prediction retraction malediction collection
— *CATION. In long words, join K and omit SHN.*
  glorification adjudication ratification
Hook on CONVEX side of CURVES.
 , or abolish; or punish
 derision , or independency.
         JOINED VOWEL SIGNS.
 joined ă; joined ĕ; joined ee; joined ĭ, ay.
after another element era illumine
 or Israel organ awful own new
 manifest or popish idemnity
         Writing Vowels to circles S, ST.
 mechanism or ministry mo-
nastic. antagonistic or or botanist
         Omission of Hooks, com, &c
 accord(ing) unfrequent right hand side
 in(con)siderate in(com)plete di(s)satisfied
 subje(c)t first (t)ime distinctive or
Words with R, L, N for the first or last consonant
 ram arm army rogue argue
 arrival rival alive live like alike
 dower dowry pair parry mar or merry
 mild mellowed mart or merit.
 name on enemy renew ruin &c
FIGURES. { 1.2.3. 4. 5. 6. 7.8.9.10. 100.1000.1000000.
            {
 100 £; 200 £; 56) 56000; 4) 400000; 10 10000000
Vowel Exhibitor. O x O.O or O for
Albert Edward Smith x or O oh; or O awe x

(See opposite page for illustrations.)

Intersection.—In expressing -*ction* (-*kshn*) the beginning part of the intersecting stroke should cross the latter part of the intersected one, for if intersected in the middle, it would, at times, be difficult to judge *which* phonograph had been first written. The vowel preceding the *c* (*k*) may be written after the intersecting letter, if required.

Hooks on convex side of curves should be sparingly used, as they require special care in writing, to preserve the form of the curve. The shortest outlines to the *eye* are not always the shortest to the *hand*. Longer outlines which may be be written with more freedom of hand, are often preferable. This remark applies to the choice of outlines generally.

Joined Vowels.—Join initial vowel in the words—across, address, afore, affluent, aggrieved, allure, annual-ly (an'l), apart, appoint, approbation, approximate, off, obsolete, obstruct, orthography, &c. Join final vowel in army, many, monarchy, &c.

Vowels written to circles S and ST.—This provision is useful when a half-length consonant precedes *s* or *st*, for according to rule on page 37A, a vowel after a halved letter would read between the primary stem and the added *n*, and not between the added *n* and the following circle.

Slope and direction of R and L.—When joined to other stroke consonants, the writer may, by a difference of inclination, indicate the relation of vowels to these letters. *Downward L* may also be thus treated when unjoined. When standing alone, or the first consonant in a word, if preceded by a first-place vowel, the *R* or *L* (downward form, if convenient) is generally written above the line; if preceded by a last-place vowel through the line. If written on the line, the downward or upward form is used, according to convenience. When *R* or *L* is the last stroke consonant in an outline, and followed by a vowel, we prefer the upstroke, unless the downstroke gives a more convenient angle for joining.

Figures.—Phonographs are briefest, particularly for high numbers requiring cyphers, but the common Arabic numerals are more conspicuous, and catch the eye better in looking over a report. "Eight" is represented by its vowel *ay* rather than by *t*, because in careless writing the latter, though differing both in length and position, might be confounded with *tn*, 10. Those who prefer the diphthongal *ayee*, (p. 66) can join upward *ee* tick to *ay*. Insert the vowel *ee* in "eighteen."

Vowel Exhibitor.—This narrow loop, to which vowels may be placed to exhibit them more distinctly, should be written thick on side, and longer than the *ss* loop. Or, two parallel strokes, ‖ or =, may be used to show vowels.

Phonetypy; or Outline Notation.—Shorthand writers have found it convenient to represent Stenographic and Phonographic characters and outlines by means of ordinary types, arranged according to peculiarities in the construction of the respective systems. In our scheme of Typic-Phonography the term *Phonegram* answers to the word *Phonograph* in written Phonography ; *Logotype*, or *Word-type* = *Word-sign* ; *Logogram* = *Logograph* ; *Phonelogue* = *Phonologue* ; and *Phraseotype* = *Phraseograph*.

Scheme :—After a letter, or cluster of letters representing a phonograph, a period is inserted. A circle occurring between two strokes, is considered to belong to the first. In the case of signs with two directions, an apostrophe indicates a downward letter ; an inverted apostrophe an upward letter. To effect a distinction between curved and straight *W*, an inverted period precedes downward straight, short *W*, and a period precedes the upward straight *W*. The position of these directive marks is suggestive of the point from which the letter is commenced ; downward letters being commenced above the line, and upward letters generally on the line. An inverted period also precedes small *F* and *V*, thin *B*, curve *T* and *D*, and the *L, R,* or *LR* added by lengthening. The "direction mark" may generally be omitted before upward, *Ry, Ly,* and downward *Kay.*   *in:* A preceding comma denotes *straight ,fr, ,vr, ,fl, ,vl.* A hyphen indicates the vowel implied by slightly lengthening *p-r, b-r, p-l, b-l,* and uncurved *f-l, v-l. S-* = initial *s* on the fore-side of a straight line ; and *-s* = final *s* on the after-side: *'st* = large circle *st; 'ss* = loop *ss ;* and *'thr* = *ther,* expressed by a second hook. A colon follows a contracted prefix, and precedes a contracted affix : when used initially, a colon represents dot *com,* or *con.* A final inverted period indicates the dot affix *ed* or *d. i* represents the *i* dash for *ing ;* when disjoined, the colon precedes. An inverted comma indicates that the phonograph which precedes it, is intersected by that which follows. *Voc.* signifies—vocalize, if time permit. Vowels, when used for vocalizing, are not separated by the period from the consonants to which they relate, but vowel word-signs should be separated. An accent (*'*) represents upward *the;* an inverted accent (*,*) down-*the. ' and,* standing alone ; *" and,* in Ph. *'a, and a ; ' l and the; i, in,* (alone and initial) but *'i* medial and final in Ph. *.i, it; wi, with ; o, of; 'oh, though ; u, unto ;* &c.

For Table of Logotypes and Grammalogues see pages 47 and 48. Except in tables, words on the line need not be marked (..)

Formation of Contractions.—After the manner of the following lists, the writer can form other Contractions and Phraseographs, according to his requirements. For instance :—*pr.p,n* for perpendicular ; *jn.rl,* general rule ; *brn mnt,* bear in mind, &c. Outlines should always be contracted by omitting the *final* or *medial* consonants, rather than an initial consonant.

⬛ny of the phonographs represented on the three following ⬛ become word-signs simply by the omission of vowels.

EXTENDED LIST OF GRAMMALOGUES, &c.

(This list includes some of the words contained in the smaller list of principal grammalogues, on page 49.)

For explanation of logotypes, see opposite page. (*) close to following word, means *above* the line; (..) *on* the line; and (₊) *through* the line.

'W,*away ..way

wr,*we are, we r ..were ₊with our

Also *w'r* in Ph. for *we are, were.*

w'r,*aware, (or join *a*) ..wear

whr,*why are ..where

wh'l,*awhile..why will. *whl**while

wl or *w'l*,*we will, we l ..will ₊well

w.t,*we ought ..wait ₊wit·

wd (*hook* and *d*) *wide, we had ..we do, widow

whd,*why had ..why do

wdnt, *we had not ..we do not (would not, in Ph.)

F, *for, half ..if ₊few. F,*n,* often

fr,*from, free ..if our. .*fr*,*offer

f'l,*feel, fall ..fail, fill ₊full

ftr,*father ..if there ₊future

·V,*have ..vow. ·*vy* ₊view

vn,*even ..vain ; join *č* for heaven

vr,..every. * ·*vr*, have our ..very

,*vr*,*over, aver ..ever, or *v.*

v'l,*evil. *v·l*,*avowal ..avail

P,*hope, happy ..up. *p'l*,*happily. *h.pl*,*haply.

pn,*happen, open ..upon, pain

pl,*apply ..play

pt,*hoped, hope it, apt ..put

pnt,*point, appoint (join *a*) ..paint

pnd,*happened, opened ..pound

B,*be ..to be, bow (to bend)

·*b*,*by, buy ..obey (*be* in Ph.)

bn,*been, combine ..to (have) been

b-r,*by our ..bear

b'l,*by all ..believe, bill

·*bt*,*about, habit. *bt*, ..but

bthr,*be there ..to be there

·*bthr*,*by their ..obey their, bidder

M,*am, me, my ..Mr., may ₊aim

mn,*man, mine ..men ₊human

mr,*more ..mere. *mr'l*, ..merely

m·l,*mile ..million. *mrn*,*more than

mp,*improve (or *mpr·v*) ..may be

N,*on, no, know ..new ₊any, now

nn,*known ..none ₊noon, join *oo*

nr,*on our, honor ..nor, near ₊inner, unr- *nrn*,*on our own.

n'l,*only, annul ..newly ₊unl-

nr'l,*nor will ..nearly ₊enrol

NG,*bang ..young, hung

nggr,*auger ..younger, hunger

ngg, ..England. *nggl*, ..English

'R,*or ..remark ₊our, hour

,*R*,*are ..remember ₊our, hurry

rr,*or our, arrear ..rare ₊error

'*rs**cars ..airs ₊ourselves

r-s*or his, arise ..arouse ₊ours, hours

'*rt*,*art, or it, aright ..writ ₊root

rt,*heart, write ● ate, wrote ₊hurt

'*rd*,*hard, ..read, (pres. tense) ₊erred

rd,*ride, rode ..read (past tense,) red ₊rude

'*rtr*,*orator. *r·tr*,*writer

'*rdr*,*order, or there ..reader

rdr,*are there, rider ..redder, ₊ruder

'*l*,*all, ..Lord, large ₊ill, ail (or *l·r* large ; *l·r j·l*, largely, &c.)

'L (written flatter), *ally, alloy ..allay, alley ₊allow

L,*law ..lay (*Lord* in Ph) ₊allow

'*l-s*,*all his ..less .'*ls*, else

[After upward L, *s* may take the "t side," and *z*, the "*d* side, to distinguish *loss* from *laws*, &c.]

ls,*loss ..lease, less ₊loose

lz,*laws, voc. lies ..lays ₊lose

'*lt*,*all it, alight ..let ₊allow it

lt,*light, lot ..let, late

'*ld*,*old, allied ..led ₊aloud, allowed

ld,*lied ..lead, laid ₊loud

'*ltr*,*alter ..letter or *ltr*

ltr,*latter, lighter ..letter, later

'*ldr*,*all their, older ..le(t) their ₊elder, allow their. *ldr*,..leader ₊louder

'Ꙁ(circle),* as, has ..is, his
'st,*as it, has it .is it (hast in Ph.)
These circles may be joined to
many word signs, taking care to let
his, is, is it always rest on the line
when joined initially. When followed by the straight lines h, y, t,
d, r, l, turn the circle on the after-
side of the stroke.
S,*see, saw ..so, say ₊us, essay
Z,*ease, easy, owes ..whose
s-wt,*as we ought. swt,*sweet
s-wd,*as we had ..as we do ₊as
would. swd,*Swede ..swayed
sb,*subject, has to be ..is to be
'stb,*has it to be ..is it to be
sm,*as may, seem, some ..same
sm·lr,*smaller ..similar
'sn,*assign, seen . hasten, soon
·sn,*h-as no, sign ..is no ₊sin
·snt,*has not ..is not, cent ₊sinned
snr,*as near ..is near ₊sinner
'su,r,*sooner. 'sꙁthn sooner than
·stnt,*has it not ..is it not
'str,*as it were ..is it our
s·l,*assail, seal ..soul, sale
s'l,*salvation ..as will ₊as well
·ss,*as has, h-as his ..is his, is : as
'ss,*assize, cease ..so has ₊essays
sz,*sees, seize ..says. s'zs,*as easy as
s'snt,*consis(t)ent, omitting one t
ts·snt,*inconsistent ..incessant
sd,*has had ..has (to) do ₊is (to) do
s-d,*side ..said ₊sued
s-dn,*sadden ..sudden
sdn,*has done ..is done
stshn,*station. s-t.shn*situation
sk,*seek ..has come ₊sake
skr,..scripture. s-kr*seeker ₊succour
s.h,*as high. s.hs..as high as
TH,*thank, I think ..think, thing
₊youth. tht*thought ..think it
thr,*author ..three ₊through
TH,*thee, thy, (that) ..them, they
₊thou. ["Though,"if represented
by a consonant word-sign, must
take the lowest position, and
the curve be deepened inPh.]

thn,*than, thine ..then ₊within
thr,*they are ..there, their ₊other,
they were   [hast
ths,*these ..this ₊thus. thst,*thou
tht,*that ..they had ₊they would
T,*at, ought ..time ₊out (to in Ph.)
tr,*at our, ought our ..true, try
₊utter. voc, or write t,r for outer
t·l,*at all ..till, tell, it will, in Ph [it
tt,*ought it. at it ..taught ₊out (of)
tthr,*at their, ought there ₊out of
their
D,*had, idea ..do ₊head, aid voc·
dr,*had our, dear ..do our, dare
dd,*had had, added ..did ₊aided
dthr,*had there ..do their ₊aid their
ddr.mn,*determine, substituting dr
hook for tr hook
chr,..which are ₊which were
chs,*choice ..which is ₊chairman's
SH,*wash, show ..should ₊wish
s.sh·l,*as shall ..social
J,*joy ..Jesus ₊age, edge. (Join
vowel for Jew')
jn,*join ..generally-ly ₊June
K,*week ..come ₊came, ache
ek.*acknowledgment ..Co. company
k·l,*call ..kill ₊cool   [to their
ek·r,*according ..ek·rthr, according
kthr,..come to their ₊came to their
ek chn,*action ..connection
k.chn,*caution. k zhn, ..occasion
Q,*quarter ..question q·l,*equal
qt,*acquit ..quite, quote ₊quit
qn,..queen. qnt,*acquaint..quantity
G,*a-go ..give ₊gave
gr,*agree ..grow ₊grew
gthr, ..give their ₊gave their
h·l,*whole ..hell, who will
hd,*ahead. hnt, . hint
hnd,*hand ..hundred
Y,*ye ..you ₊yea
yr,*year ..your ₊you were
y·l,*ye will ..you will yr·l,*yearly
yt,*ye ought ..yet. ynt,..you not
yd,*ye had ..you had ₊you would
bynd,*beyond. yntr,*yonder
ys, ..yes ₊use. ys.f·l, useful

The *(up or down)*	will (noun)	part	down
and	h-our	had	human
of	him	out	a-go
to *or* in Ph.	on	every	large
in	there	unto	Christianity
a an	at	great -ness	Chairman
that *or*	more	one	England
is his	what	her	English
it *or* t Ph.	God *or* Ph.	most	principle
its *or* 6 Ph.	who *or* c	must	probable
I, eye	whom	world	improbable
with	than *,* then	into	perfect
for	so	was	imperfect
you	thy ee thou	were *or*	opportunity
be — been —	word	where	first *or*
as has	Lord *for*	do done	high
he *or* Ph.	upward L Ph	give-n	general
but	Jesus	gave	consider
are (up)	shall	these	year
not	should	ever *or*	ought
have	how	under	over
which	if	well	few *or*
all	those Ph	come came	new
from	no, know	spirit	child
your	any *or*	thing	thank
or *(down)*	when	now	why
by	can	though	away
this	cannot	very	way
we *or* Ph.	would	nor	young
them	up — upon —	near	youth
me	us	am	without *for* y
will *I or*	other	yet	wicked (up)
or L in Ph.	Mr. may	too *or*	&c.

LOCOGRAPHS, or Contracted Outlines, arranged alphabet^y

According	inconvenient	plenipotentiary
applicability	inconsistency	probability
bankrupt	indispensable	proportionate
Cabinet	individual	questionable
characteristic	insignificant	reform
circumstance	insignificance	respectively
defendant	intelligent *or*	regeneration
disadvantage	intellectual	remarkable *or*
discharge	insufficient	represent
disrespectful	irrespective	respect
dissatisfaction	irresponsible	resurrection
distinguish	Jurisprudence	retrospect
establish	manufacture	satisfaction
establishment	Methodism	satisfactory *or*
evangelical	misdemeanour	sensibility
expect	Nonconformist	suspect 2 *or*
expectation	object	scepticism
expenditure	objectionable	straightforward
extraordinary	objective	thanksgiving
extravagant	parliament-ary	transubstantiation
gentleman	peculiarity	unexpectedly
impracticable	perform	uniformity
improbability	plaintiff *or*	wonderful 2
		hook omitted

Outlines. Punctuation, &c.

(The dotted signs may be omitted.)

Aristocracy	hydrogen	peculiar
article	or	impregnable	perpetual
chapter	imperturbable	popular
constitute	indenture	Post office order
contentment	influential	Protestant
commercial	institute	Principality
danger	insubordination	recognisance
dignity	intemperance	receiver or
discourse	interest	remembrance
disfranchise	magistrate	sensible
Episcopalian	mechanic	sufficient
essential	messenger	substantial
excommunicate	mortgage	tribunal
exchequer	mortgagee	universe or
executor	metropolis	until
extinguish	necessary	verbatim or
extra	necessity or	yesterday
financial	observation	DAYS:-
forgery	Omnipotent	
friend	orthodox-y	Sunday or

MONTHS.

STOPS:- Comma Semicolon Colon Period. // see p 53
Interrogation ! Exclamation Laughter = Hyphen
Dash, or Italics — First letter capital Lord

Circles thus formed are equivalent to "s and hook" loops. persuade

DISTINGUISHING

Words containing OF the same consonants.

void — avoid — evade — available — valuable

in fact — in effect — physical — fiscal

forward — froward — farther — further — Free —

offer — hopes — peace — comparison — person

prison — pattern — patron — stable — suit-

able — special-ly — especial-ly — separate-ly

support — spirit — opposition — position —

or — possession — perhaps — propose — [pose
                                          pur-

need — end — amiable — humble — many

money — amaze — amuse — nobody — any-

body — nothing — or — anything — truly — utterly

altitude — or — latitude — Trinity — eternity

train — horn — difference — or — deference

audit — edit — auditor — auditory — editor —

daughter — debtor — adversity — diversity

gentle — genteel — cost — or — caused — or —

accused — occupy — keep — guidance — or —

goodness — or — gradual-ly — greatly — quite
                                             [it

quiet — acute — Creator — creature — quarter

responsible — or — irresponsible

moral — or — immoral; — mor-
                              [tal

or — immortal — numerable — [in
                                  u-

measurable — im-

NOTICES.

As a matter of justice to ourselves, and those who write, and will write, this system, we deem it our duty before going to press with this, our last sheet, to give the following Mems:—In the Phonetic Journal for September 27th, 1862, Mr. I. Pitman, after condemning his method of representing *CH* and downward *R*, proposed, as a greatly superior arrangement, to write *R* by a sloping straight line written upwards, or downwards. *We used this plan in a phonetic alphabet, upwards of a year before this date.* A few weeks later, in one weekly number of the Journal, the three following ideas were published:—(1) The adding of *r* to the generality of the letters of the alphabet by an initial hook. (2) The adding of *l* by a large initial hook, and (3) Adding *L* by lengthening curves. *We had then used Nos.* 1 *and* 2 *more than a year*, and Mr. Pitman possessed information that they had been used by us so long ago. *No.* 3 *we had used nearly a year* to lessen the work of the large initial hooks, and although we requested Mr. Pitman, as a matter of common fairness, to mention this circumstance in his Phonetic Journal, and to correct an erroneous apprehension arising from a remark on p. 706, vol. 21, he has hitherto declined to do so. This being the case, and not knowing what alterations Mr. Pitman may ultimately adopt in a future edition, we have given the above particulars in this Handbook. Want of space prevents our giving the correspondence between us.

PHONIC SHORTHAND SOCIETY.—To assist Students, by free correction of Exercises through the post, and to afford facilities for intercommunication between writers of this system, those who acquire proficiency in its use, and wish to further the above objects, are invited to forward a shorthand note to the author, with name and address in longhand, and, all being well, on the 1st July, 1863, a printed list will be published of names received. This list may be obtained on application by Shorthand note, (Learners', or advanced style,) enclosing a *stamped, addressed envelope*. The list will be enlarged and revised from time to time, and changes of residence should be at once communicated. No charge for membership; expenses being defrayed by voluntary contributions. For exercises, Students should write from twelve to twenty verses of Scripture, on alternate lines, and forward to a member for correction, with *stamped, addressed envelope*, for return.

Stops.—See page 51. " , ; : . " as usual, or, a small cross may be written, or about $\frac{3}{4}$ inch space left, for a full stop. The dot will preserve a space between sentences. In the Reading Exercises, a cross is used. When used to denote an initial Capital, the small cross should be written close, like a vowel.

Two sloping parallel strokes, struck upwards, or downwards, (see page 51) separate speeches, or remarks of different persons, as questions and answers, in reporting testimony in a court of law, &c.

SPEECH OF LORD CHATHAM, IN THE HOUSE OF PEERS, AGAINST THE AMERICAN WAR, AND AGAINST EMPLOYING THE INDIANS IN IT.

(Key to Reading Exercise on page 75, &c.)

I cannot, my lords, I will not, join in congratulation on misfortune and disgrace. This, my lords, is a perilous and tremendous moment. It is not a time for adulation: the smoothness of flattery cannot save us in this rugged and awful crisis. It is now necessary to instruct the throne in the language of truth. We must, if possible, dispel the delusion and darkness which envelope it, and display, in its full danger and genuine colours, the ruin which is brought to our doors. Can ministers still presume to expect support in their infatuation? Can parliament be so dead to its dignity and duty, as to give their support to measures thus obtruded and forced upon them? Measures, my lords, which have reduced this late flourishing empire to scorn and contempt! "But yesterday, and Britain might have stood against the world ; now, none so poor as to do her reverence." The people, whom we at first despised as rebels, but whom we now acknowledge as enemies, are abetted against us, supplied with every military store, have their interests consulted, and their ambassadors entertained, by our inveterate enemy—and ministers do not, and dare not interpose, with dignity or effect. The desperate state of our army abroad is in part known. No man more highly esteems and honours the British troops than I do ; I know their virtues and their valour ; I know they can achieve anything but impossibilities ; and I know *(page 76)* that the conquest of British America is an impossibility. You cannot, my lords, you cannot conquer America. What is your present situation there? We do not know the *worst;* but we know that in three campaigns we have done nothing, and suffered much. You may swell every expense, accumulate every assistance, and extend your traffic to the shambles of every German despot: your attempts will be for ever vain and impotent—doubly so, indeed, from this mercenary aid on which you rely; for it irritates, to an incurable resentment, the minds of your adversaries, to overrun them with the mercenary sons of rapine and plunder, devoting them and their possessions to the rapacity of hireling cruelty. If I were an American as I am an Englishman, while a foreign troop was landed in my country, I never would lay down my arms—never, never, never!

But, my lords, who is the man that, in addition to the disgraces and mischiefs of the war, has dared to authorise and associate to our arms the tomahawk and scalping-knife of the savage ?—to call into civilized alliance the wild and inhuman inhabitant of the woods ? — to delegate to the merciless Indian the defence of disputed rights, and to wage the horrors of this barbarous war against our brethren? My lords, these enormities cry aloud for redress and punishment. But, my lords, this barbarous measure has been defended, not only on the principles of policy and necessity, but also on those of morality;

"for it is perfectly allowable," says Lord Suffolk, "to use all the means which God and nature have put into our hands." I am astonished, I am shocked, to hear such principles confessed; to hear them avowed in this house, or in this country. My lords, I did not intend to encroach so much on your attention, but I cannot repress my indignation—I feel myself impelled to speak. My lords, we are called upon as *(page 77)* members of this house, as men, as Christians, to protest against such horrible barbarity!—"That God and nature have put into our hands!" What ideas of God and nature that noble lord may entertain, I know not; but I know, that such detestable principles are equally abhorrent to religion and humanity. What! to attribute the sacred sanction of God and nature to the massacres of the Indian scalping-knife! to the cannibal savage, torturing, murdering, devouring, drinking the blood of his mangled victims! Such notions shock every precept of morality, every feeling of humanity, every sentiment of honour. These abominable principles, and this more abominable avowal of them, demand the most decisive indignation.

I call upon that right reverend, and this most learned bench, to vindicate the religion of their God, to support the justice of their country. I call upon the bishops to interpose the unsullied sanctity of their lawn; upon the judges, to interpose the purity of their ermine, to save us from this pollution. I call upon the honour of your lordships, to reverence the dignity of your ancestors, and to maintain your own. I call upon the spirit and humanity of my country, to vindicate the national character. I invoke the *genius of the constitution*. From the tapestry that adorns these walls, the immortal ancestor of this noble lord frowns with indignation at the disgrace of his country. In vain did he defend the liberty, and establish the religion of Britain, against the tyranny of Rome, if these worse than popish cruelties, and inquisitorial practices, are endured among us. To send forth the merciless cannibal, thirsting for blood! against whom?—your Protestant brethren!—to lay waste their country, to desolate their dwellings, and extirpate their race and name, by the aid and instrumentality of these horrible hounds of war! Spain can no longer boast pre-eminence in barbarity. She armed herself with blood-hounds, to extirpate *(page 78)* the wretched natives of Mexico; we, more ruthless, loose these dogs of war against our countrymen in America, endeared to us by every tie that can sanctify humanity. I solemnly call upon your lordships, and upon every order of men in the state, to stamp upon this infamous procedure the indelible stigma of the public abhorrence. More particularly, I call upon the holy prelates of our religion to do away this iniquity; let them perform a lustration, to purify the country from this deep and deadly sin. My lords, I am old and weak, and at present unable to say more; but my feelings and indignation were too strong to have said less. I could not have slept this night in my bed, nor even reposed my head upon my pillow, without giving vent to my eternal abhorrence of such enormous and preposterous principles.

Mems :—Phraseographs should be suggestive; should consist of words which frequently occur together in speech, and between which a relation exists. The outlines of a phrase should join easily, and not straggle too far from the line, else, it is better to lift the pen. Unimportant words may be omitted, and occasionally, the omission may be indicated by writing the other words closer. Exs:— ₊*tˡ* out (of) the; *mbn* may (have) been; | | time (after) time; || day (after) day; *wn mst*, (joined, or detached) one (of the) most, &c. See lists.

PHRASEOGRAMS. KEY TO OPPOSITE PAGE.

1. A great extent	As if there had	By the
2. A long time	As it may be	By which there will
3. According to the......	As it has been	Can be; cannot be
4. According to agreement...	As it should be	Chancellor of the Exchequer.
5. Act of Parliament	As long as	Children of God.
6. Acts of Parliament......	As many as possible	Christian religion.
7. Again and again......	As much as	Church and state.
8. All it	As soon as	Church of England.
9. All its bearings	As the; as to......	Church of God.
10. All that has been said ...	As usual......	Circumstantial evidence.
11. And h-as; and h-is	As well as possible --	Court of Bankruptcy.
12. And a; and I......	At all times	Court of Chancery.
13. And in; and the......	At all events......	Court of Common Pleas.
14. And he; and it	At last; at least	Court of justice.
15. And for which......	At the same time	Court of Queen's Bench.
16. And have; and should ...	Attorney general	Courts of law
17. And when there	Between them	Everlasting life.
18. Are there......	Between their	Every consideration
19. Are you sure	But it has been	For Christ's sake.
20. As far as......	But this......	For ever and ever.
21. As fast as	But which......	For he
22. As good as	But you......	For instance.
23. As great as	By all means......	For It should
24. As a; as he; as in......	By our	For it has been much

Phraseographs.

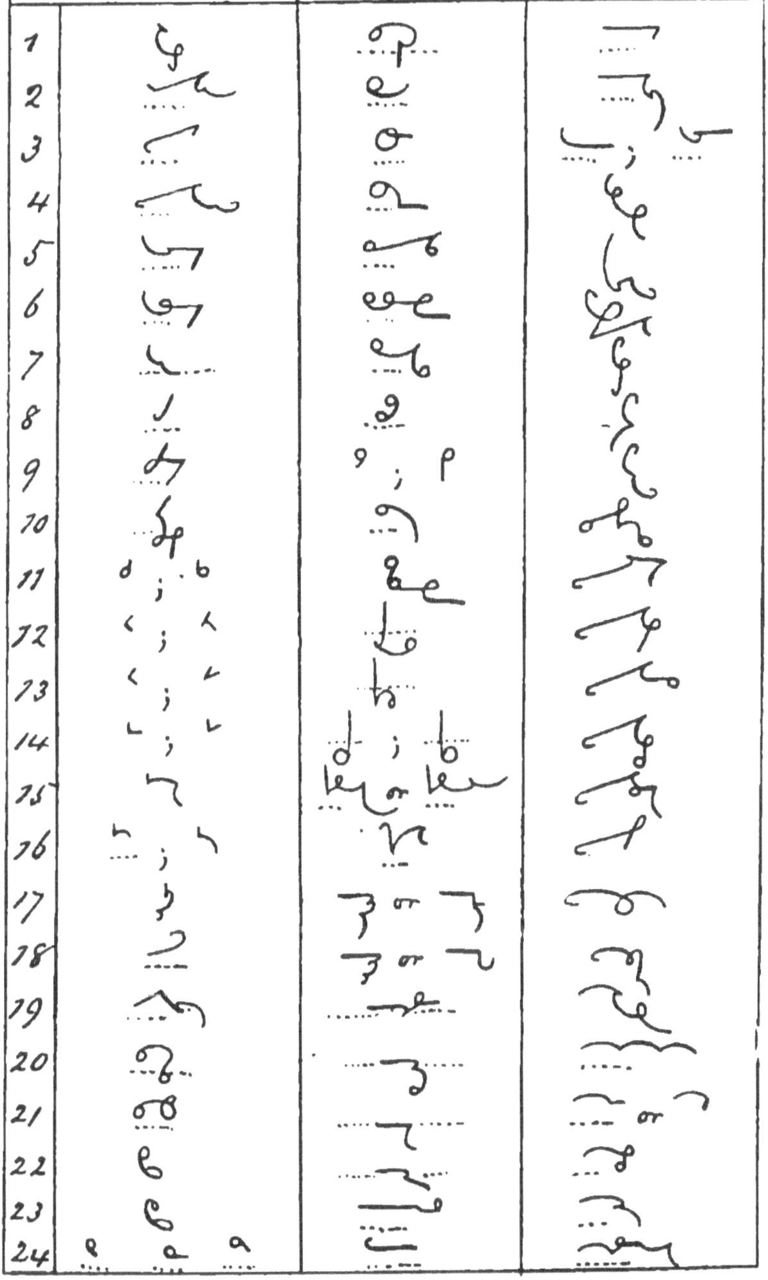

1			
2			
3			
4			
5			
6			
7			
8			
9			
10			
11			
12			
13			
14			
15			
16			
17			
18			
19			
20			
21			
22			
23			
24			

Suggestive Signs.—A common business "&c.," with *c* joined, may stand for the remainder of a familiar text or quotation. Write a capital "I" when the remarks of a speaker are, for a time, Inaudible.

A cross (consonant size) implies error; if on the part of the speaker, join *s* to the last stroke.

Doubt as to the correctness of a word, sentence, or remark, is shown by a large interrogation mark.

Write the usual caret (∧) for an omission, and leave space according to its extent.

Divisions, or heads of a discourse, may be separated by two small crosses.

PHRASEOGRAMS. KEY TO OPPOSITE PAGE.

1. For such as are	He has (or is) not............	I am quite certain
2. For the most part	He should	I believe
3. For the purpose of..........	He was; he will	I can do
4. For the sake of	Hear, hear....................	I cannot see
5. For they will be......	Her Majesty's Government.	I will not expect
6. For their; for their own.	Holy Ghost	I do; I had
7. For this reason	Holy Scriptures..............	I do not think
8. For those who are..........	Holy Spirit	I expect
9. For which; for your	Honorable gentleman	I had not given
10. Freedom of the press	Hon. and gallant member...	I have been told there
11. From my, or me............	Hon. and learned friend ...	I have done
12. From time to time	House of Commons	I have no doubt
13. From which; from whom.	House of God........	I hope you are satisfied
14. Future state	House of Lords	I know there is
15. Generation to generation..	House of Parliament.........	I may as well
16. Generation after generation	Houses of Parliament	I must be
17. Great advantage............	House of prayer..............	I need not reply
18. Gentlemen of the jury ...	House of representatives ...	I shall feel
19. Greater than	How are you.................	I think I shall not
20. Have been; have had ...	How many....................	I will not make
21. Have felt	How should	I wish there had been
22. Have you	How will	If it is (or has) not
23. Heavenly Father	Human nature	If I
24. He has been	I agree with the	If the case

Suggestive Signs.—Leading remarks may be made conspicuous by the usual marginal strokes, or longhand *n* for "Note."

An Outline or Phrasecograph to which the reporter wishes to refer at leisure, should be encircled. Prominence may thus be given either to incorrect outlines, or to specially good ones which occur to the writer for the first time. Of the latter, a memorandum should be kept.

Texts.—Write first the No. of Book, or Epistle, then name of Book or Epistle; No. of Chapter, or Psalm, above the line, and Verse, or verses, on the line.

Mem.—In addition to distinction by thickness, write the dash for the Grammalogue "*a*" more perpendicularly than that for "*in*."

PHRASEOGRAMS. KEY TO OPPOSITE PAGE.

1	If there is (or has) not*	In the last place	Lord Chancellor.
2	If there is to be	In the sight of God	Lord Chief Justice.
3	If we are not	In the way	Lords and Commons.
4	If we were not	In the word of God	Many more
5	In a great measure	In the world	Many such
6	In all respects	Is it the	More and more
7	In comparison	Is it not so	More than
8	In connection (with)	It is a well known fact	My brethren.
9	In consequence (of)	It is most important	My beloved brethren.
10	In fact	It is not necessary	My Christian friends.
11	In its	It is quite certain that it cannot be brought	My dear sir.
12	In his opinion		My fellow townsmen.
13	In no case	It seems to be	Mr. Chairman.
14	In any case	It should not	Mr. Speaker.
15	In our	It would have been	National reform.
16	In order to give	Justice of the peace	Notwithstanding the
17	In reference (to)	Justification by faith	Nor will there
18	In regard (to)	Ladies and gentlemen	Of his own
19	In relation (to)	Law of the land	Of importance
20	In respect (to)	Laws of God	Of it; of its
21	In such a manner that	Learned counsel	Of many of them
22	In the first place	Learned friend	Of such as have
23	In the next place	Liberty of the press. [Christ	Of those who are
24	In the second place	Lord and Saviour Jesus	Of the

* In this, and a few other phrases, write *t* hook as a contraction for *not*.

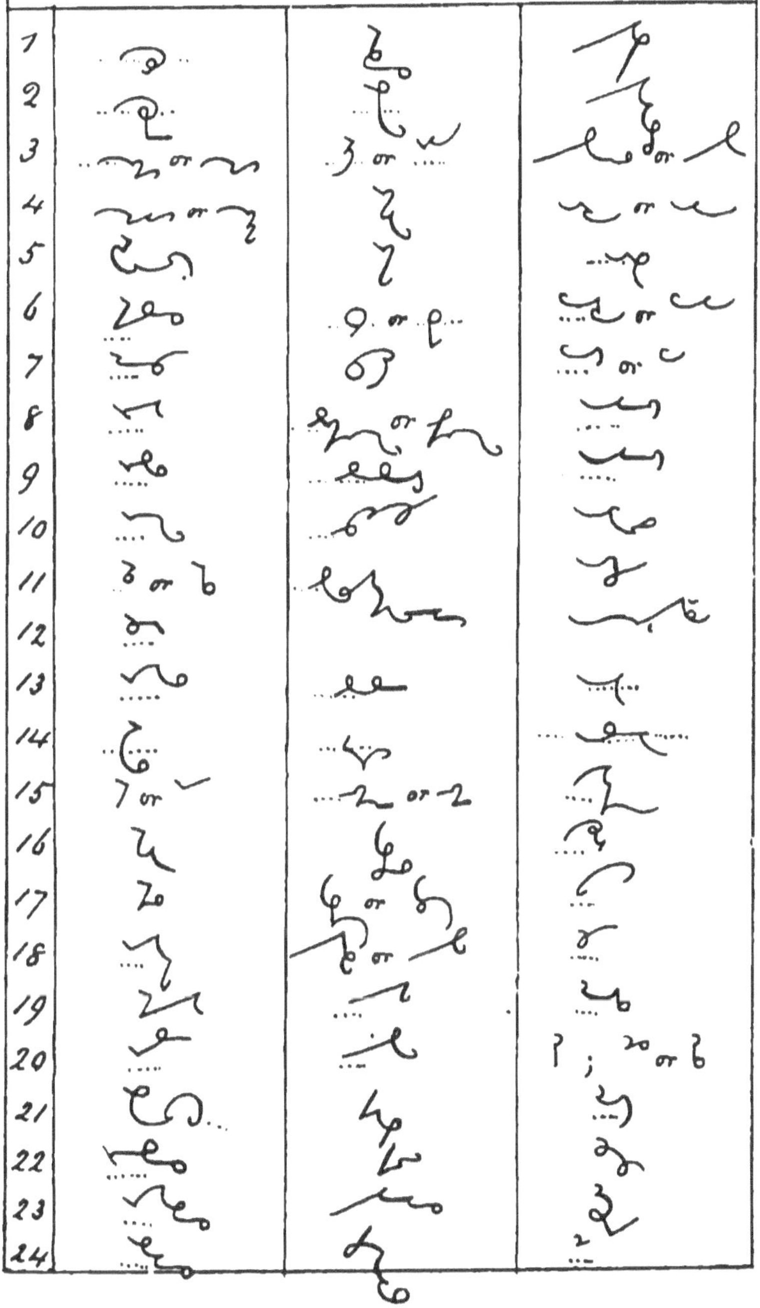

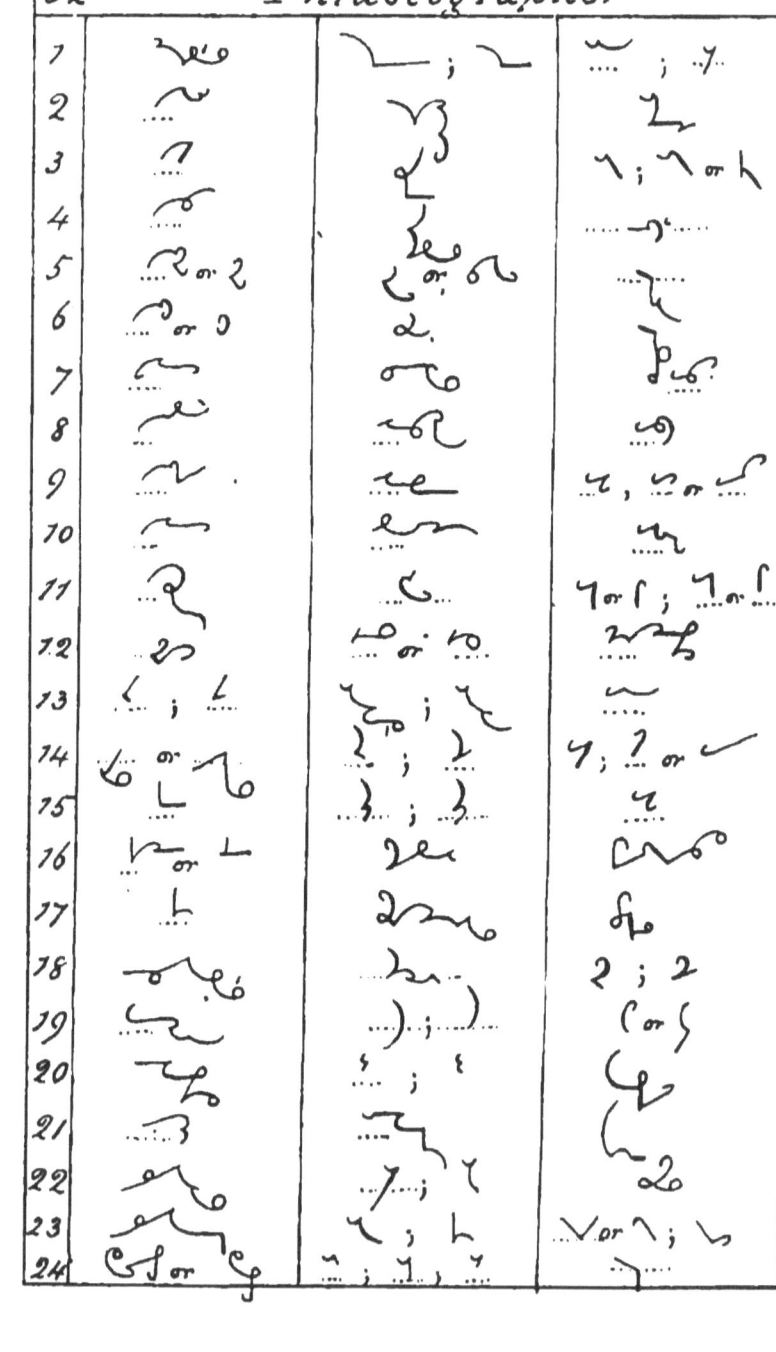

M.S. Circulating Magazines.—Familiarity with outlines is greatly furthered by one phonographer reading the handwriting of others, by correspondence, interchange of literary articles, or M.S. Circulating Magazines, managed as follows:—The conductor receives articles, written on paper of uniform size, from a staff of about a dozen members, and a number of these articles (in the handwriting of the members), together with the title-page, editorial remarks, blank space for remarks by members on outlines, &c., are bound in magazine form, weighing 3 to 3½ ounces, and forwarded under cover, open at the ends, by 1d. book post, from member to member, as per postal list of names and addresses inserted in the magazine.

PHRASEOGRAMS.   KEY TO OPPOSITE PAGE.

1. Of which it seems	Shall be; should be	To me, or my; to our
2. On account of their	Should not think that	To think about the
3. On all.........................	So as to be.....................	To you; to your
4. On his own....................	So that it is impossible......	Upon their
5. On the one hand.............	Son of God....................	United Kingdom
6. On the other hand............	Sons of men	United States.
7. On our part	Spirit of Christ..............	Was not
8. On the same	The present time	Was there
9. On the contrary	The prisoner at the bar......	We are not
10. On the part of	The same point of view......	We did not intend
11. On this occasion............	The great	We do; we had
12. One another	The first.....................	We have not observed
13. Or a; or the	Take place; take care	We may
14. Our text....................	That he; that the.............	We will
15. Ought to be	That we; that would [case.	We will not
16. Ought not to be [the case.	There are some who. [case.	What are your reasons?
17. Ought to have. [the case.	There is another view of the	What is the difference?
18. Peculiar circumstances of	They have had many	When he; when the
19. Political economy	They will; that will..........	Which are [dered
20. Public service..............	Though the; though there...	Which may be consi-
21. Rather than	To be able to show	Which will have been
22. Resurrection of Christ ...	To all our; to which.........	Ways and means
23. Resurrection of the body..	To give; to have.............	Who are
24. Secretary of state	To him; to it; to the	Who do

We shall be glad to receive particulars of magazines, and names of conductors, to publish along with the list of writers, referred to on page 53. Bordered magazine paper may be obtained, post free, in five quire packets, at 2s. to 2s. 6d., from Mr. J. B. De Voto, Lithographer, 36, Montrose-street, Glasgow.

It has been suggested that a lithographed periodical is desirable for reading practice We are obliged for the suggestion, and, in time, it will probably be carried out.

PHRASEOGRAMS. KEY TO OPPOSITE PAGE.

1.	Who had been	With the opinion	Would a
2.	Who have had	With that	Would be
3.	Who may	With them	Would have given
4.	Who will	With this, or these	Would he
5.	Who will not	With which it may be	Would not
6.	Will be	With whom there	Would our
7.	Will have	With your	Would the
8.	Will not be	Without his knowledge	Would there
9.	Will there, or their	Without it	Would this
10.	Will this	Without our	Would they
11.	Will they	Without such	Would you require
12.	Wisdom of God	Without the	You are
13.	With a few	Without their	You are not
14.	With advantage	Word of God	You had; you may
15.	With his	Words of the text	You ought; you ought [not
16.	With him	Words of my text	You should
17.	With it	Words of our text	You were
18.	With its own	Works of God	You will have been
19.	With me, or my	Works of the law	Yes my Lord
20.	With our	Working men	Your Honor
21.	With reference to	World to come	Your Lordship
22.	With regard to	Worse and worse	Your Worship
23.	With respect to	Worth while	Your own
24.	With such	Worthy friend	Yours truly

Errata.—An *h* omitted in "*diphthŏng*," foot-note, page 14.

In a few copies, ⌒ is printed instead of ⌣ in the word *Timothy*, page 79. Please correct with pen.

1			
2			
3			
4			
5			
6			
7			
8			
9			
10			
11			
12			
13			
14			
15			
16			
17			
18			
19			
20			
21			
22			
23			
24			

Diphthongs.

Manner of forming various Monosyllabic and Dissyllabic diphthongs, English, provincial English, and Foreign.

---

note:— [shorthand symbols]

"e" is used for the vowel in "men".

DOT vowels for first element.

Monosyllabic:—

[shorthand] ă ee / e ee = I [shorthand] hī / hĕ ee [shorthand] āh ee, as in aye, yes) [shorthand] ah oo / e oo

Dissyllabic:—

[shorthand] a·e / e·a [shorthand] or [shorthand] a·ee / a·i [shorthand] e·ee / e·i or [shorthand] e·ee / e·i [shorthand] a·aw / a·uh [shorthand] e·aw / e·uh [shorthand] a·oh / a·oo

[shorthand] e·oh / e·oo [shorthand] a i [shorthand] e·i etc.

DASH vowel for first element.

Monosyllabic:—

[shorthand] Welsh long u [shorthand] ayee. The diphthongal pronunciation of ay which Webster describes as ay with an ee "vanish."

DASH vowel initial. Dissyllabic :—

[shorthand symbols] *ee-a / i-a* [shorthand] *ee-e / i-e* [shorthand] *ay-i* [shorthand] *i-ee* [shorthand] *i-ay* [shorthand] *ay-ee*

[shorthand symbols] *ee-aw / ee-uh* [shorthand] *i-aw / i-uh* [shorthand] *ay-aw / ay-uh* [shorthand] *ee-oh / ee-uh* [shorthand] *i-oh / French u* [shorthand] *ay-oh / ay-oo*

[shorthand symbols] *ee-i* [shorthand] *i-i* [shorthand] *ay-i* [shorthand] *ee-ow* [shorthand] *i-ow* [shorthand] *ay-ow &c.*

AW, UH ; for the first element.

Monosyllabic :—

[shorthand] *aw-ee / uh-ee* = *OI* [shorthand] *hoi / huh-ee* [shorthand] *aw-oo / uh-oo* = *OU*

Dissyllabic :—

[shorthand] *aw-a / uh-a* [shorthand] *aw-e / uh-e* [shorthand] *aw-ee / uh-ee* [shorthand] *aw-i / uh-i* [shorthand] *aw-ay / uh-ay* [shorthand] *aw-i / uh-i &c.*

OH, OO ; for first element.

Monosyllabic :—

[shorthand] *oh-ee / oo-ee* = *French OUI* [shorthand] *oh-ee / oo-ee* [shorthand] *ohoo OH with oo "varied".*

Dissyllabic :—

[shorthand] *oh-a / oo-a* [shorthand] *oh-e / oo-e* [shorthand] *oh-ee / oo-ee* [shorthand] *oh-i / oo-i* [shorthand] *oh-ay / oo-ay* [shorthand] *oh-ow / oo-ow* = *French OI.*

[shorthand] *oh-i* [shorthand] *Ohio* ? ? *&c.*

I for first element. [shorthand] *i-a / i-e* [shorthand] *i-ee* [shorthand] *i-i* [shorthand] *i-ay* [shorthand] *i-oh &c.*

OI for first element. [shorthand] *oi-a* [shorthand] *oi-ee* [shorthand] *oi-i* [shorthand] *oi-ay &c.*

OW for first element. [shorthand] *ow-a / ow-e* [shorthand] *ow-ee* [shorthand] *ow-i* [shorthand] *ow-ay &c.*

U (roo) for first element. [shorthand] *u-a / u-e* [shorthand] *u-ee* [shorthand] *u-i* [shorthand] *u-ay &c.* [shorthand] *u-oh / u-uh*

[row of shorthand symbols] *w, h, y*

[row of shorthand symbols]

[row of shorthand symbols] x

Foreign Sounds not provided for in other parts of this work.

French Nasals. — We have furnished both a vowel and a consonant representation for French Nasality. The vowel-signs are modifications of the signs for the simple un-nasalised vowels. A difference of opinion existing as to whether the vowel sound heard in "pain" (bread) is nasalised ã or ẽ, we have given this sound the *middle* of the consonant: it thus lies between the two.

The nasal sounds are given in the order in which they are generally found in French grammars.

Nasalised

1) ã or ẽ •| represented in French by   in}, ain}
                                                  im}, aim}

2) Short aw °| „   „   „   „   an}, en}
                                                  am}, em}

3) „ oh °| „   „   „   „   on, om

4) UH •o| „   „   „   „   un, um

The diphthongal nasal *ien* is expressed by ⁶| .

The signs Nos 2 and 4 are **commenced** like ⌐ ⌐ ; No 3 like ⌐ ⌐ . The side first written with downward motion, should be thicker than the other. To indicate a longer vowel, write the circles a little larger.

Consonant signs for Nasality. S down ╱ upward ╲

With the consonant signs the ordinary vowels are used.

Guttural CH, heard in Scotch, Irish, Welsh and German, is expressed by " ⊂ ", thickened Q sign.

In German, " ⊃ " may be used as an additional sign for CH, and " ⊃ " for the fellow German guttural G. If written with too slight a curve, no confusion will arise,) th) th not being required in German.

GERMAN W, a softened pronunciation of V, between English V and W may be represented by English V or by " ⊃ " joined.

Aspirated R, (Welsh RH.) ⟨ down, or ⌒

Aspirated or Whispered L. (Welsh LL) ⟨ or ⌒

For aspirated M, N, the curve is deepened. ⌣ ⌒ .

The strengthening of letters, as required in Oriental languages, is expressed by intersection with a wavy dash. ✗ or ⤬ , ✚ , ✗ or ✗ ✗ &c.

The indistinct French vowel heard final in "libre, peuple &c" may be expressed by " ⟩ " as ⤻ ⤻. The same sign may be employed to indicate the obscure vowel supposed by some to precede the last consonant of such English words as "people, able, battle, written &c" ⤻ , ⤸ . ⌐ , ⤸ &c.

In writing foreign languages, the facilities which this system affords for representing "vowel words" and for joining vowels to each other, and to preceding or following consonants, will be found very convenient.

MEDIUM or NEUTRAL VOWELS.

When the required vowel sound is strictly nei-ther that of a first nor last place vowel, but lies be-tween the two, the sign may be written to the **middle** of the consonant accordingly.

Ex :— In words ending in -tion, -sion, -ton, -don, &c, the accepted pronunciation is neither ⟨ shon, nor ⟩ shun, but a vowel sound hitherto unexpressed in phonetic writing or printing. In accordance with these ideas, we should write ⤸ station

The vowel in the words "bad, that" in the mouth of a Londoner is neither ă nor ĕ, but a modification of the two, and may be represented by writing the dot to the middle of the consonant, half-way between ă and ĕ, when great exactitude is required.

ACCENT

may be shown, when necessary, by writing the accented vowel to **touch** the phonograph to which it relates.

⤻ convert, ⤴ convért; ⤸ convict, ⤴ convíct.
   noun   verb;   noun   verb.

Reading Exercises.

Psalm XXVII.

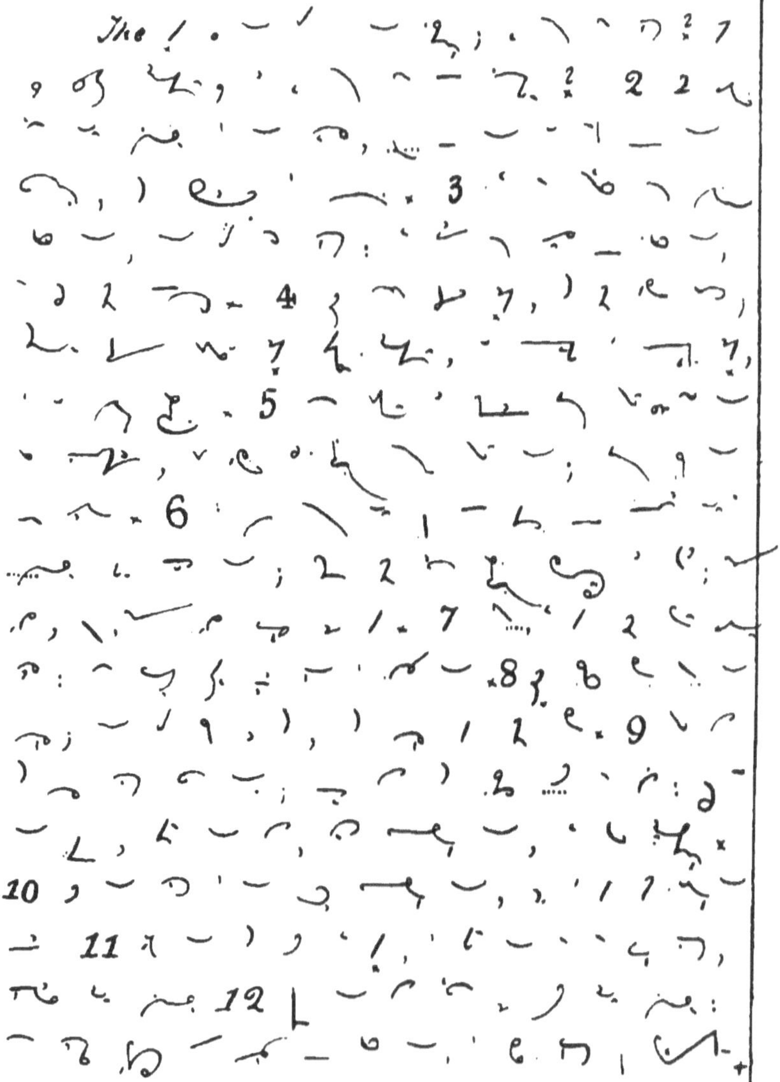

13 [shorthand]

14 [shorthand]

[shorthand]

Proverbs. Chap. XXV.

These [shorthand] 2, [shorthand]

[shorthand] 2 [shorthand]

[shorthand] 3 [shorthand]

[shorthand] 4 [shorthand]

[shorthand] 5 [shorthand]

[shorthand] 6 [shorthand]

[shorthand]

7 [shorthand]

[shorthand]

8 [shorthand] 2 6 [shorthand]

[shorthand] 9 [shorthand]

[shorthand] 10 6

[shorthand]

11 [shorthand]

12 [shorthand]

[shorthand] 7 13 [shorthand]

[shorthand] 9

14 [shorthand]

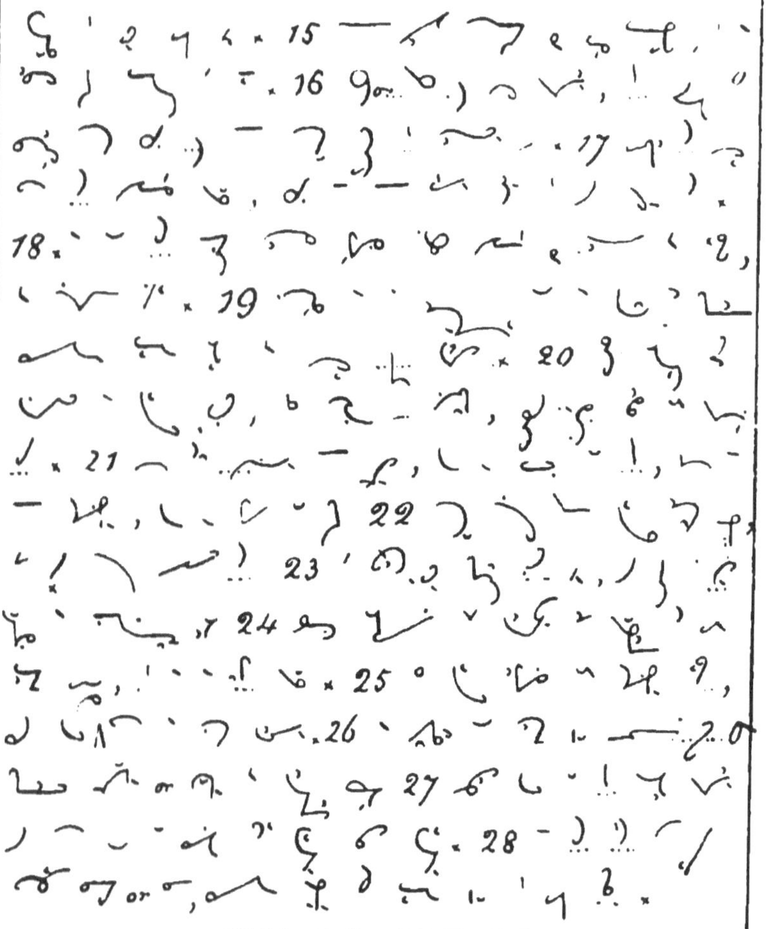

PAUL'S *declamation before* AGRIPPA.

ACTS XXVI.

Then

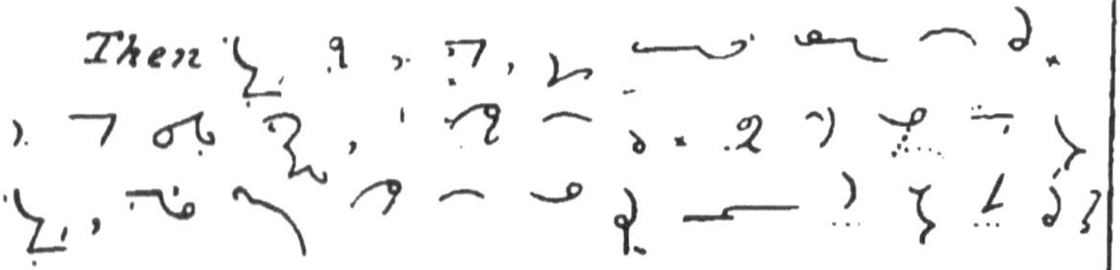

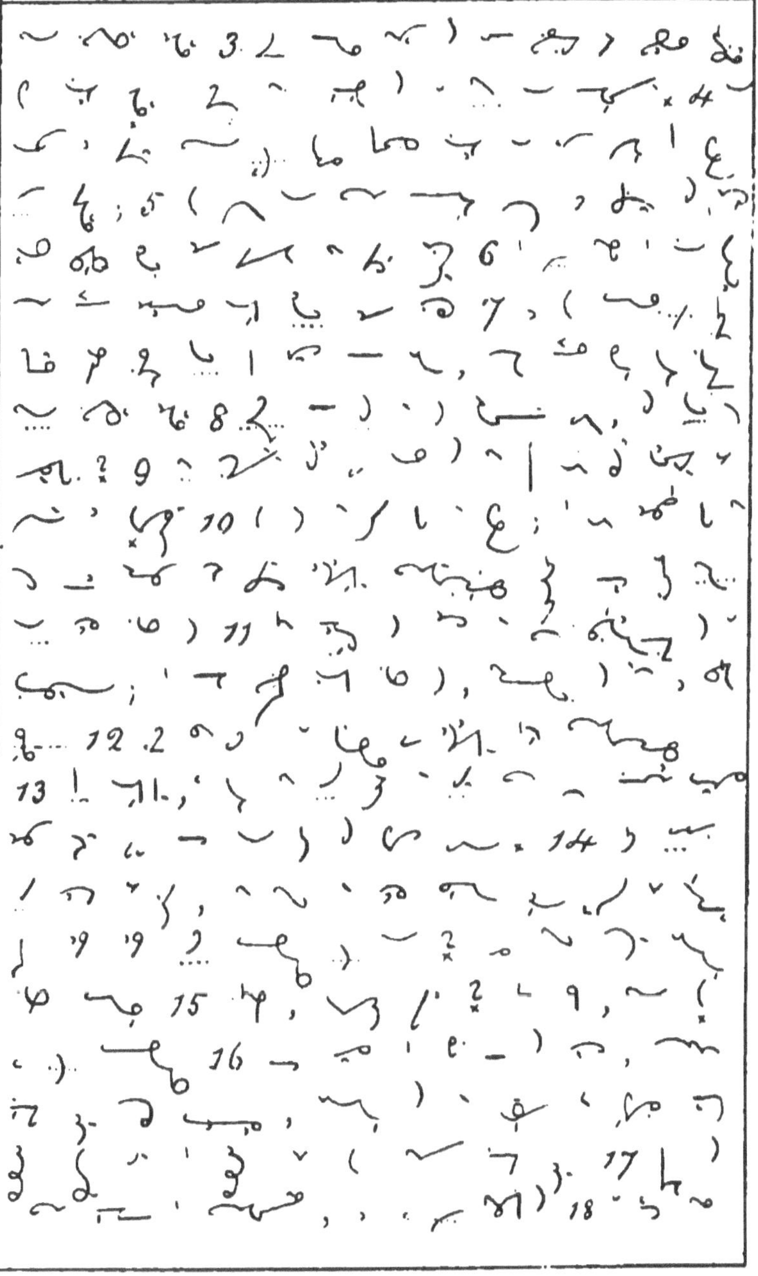

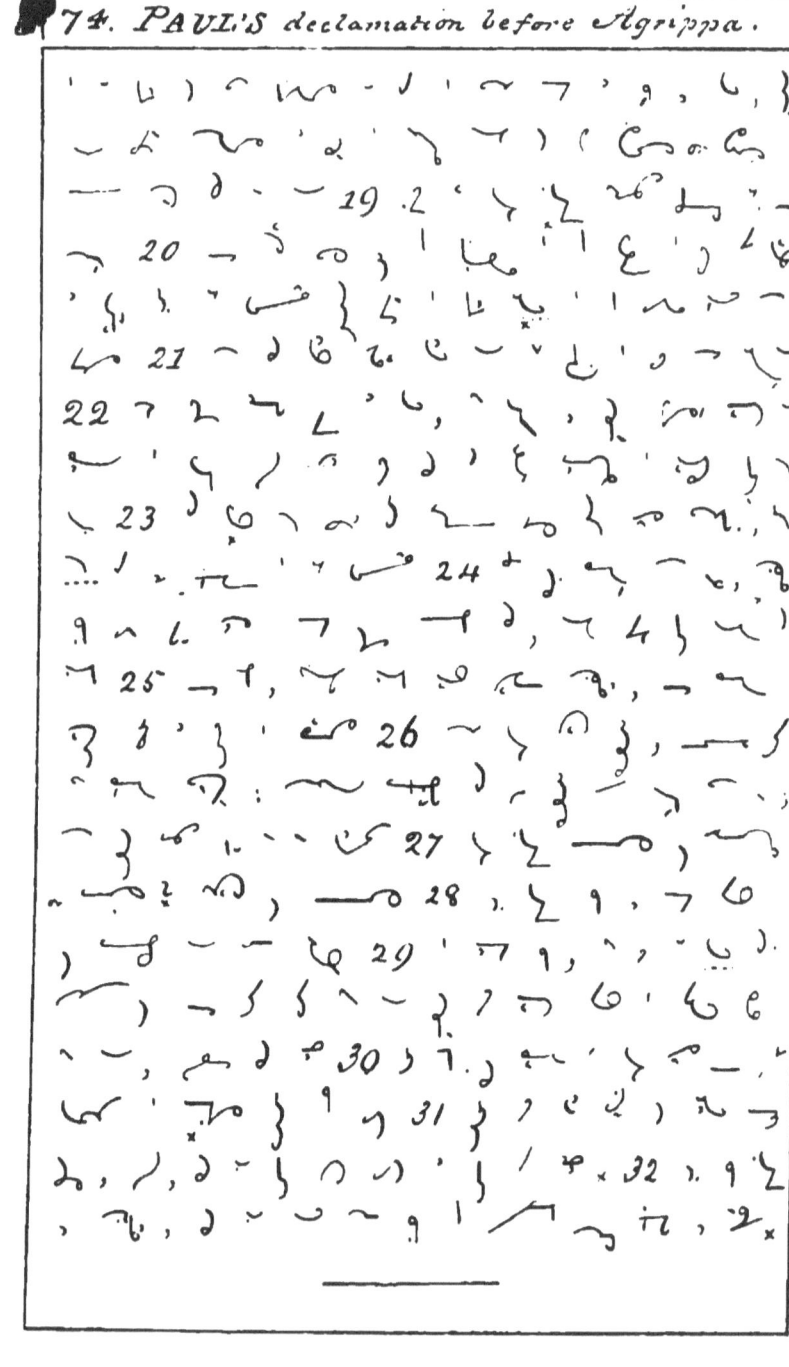

Speech of Lord Chatham

in the House of Peers against the American War, and against employing the
Indians in it.

(From Chambers's principles of Elocution.)

76. *Reading Exercise. Speech of Lord Chatham.*

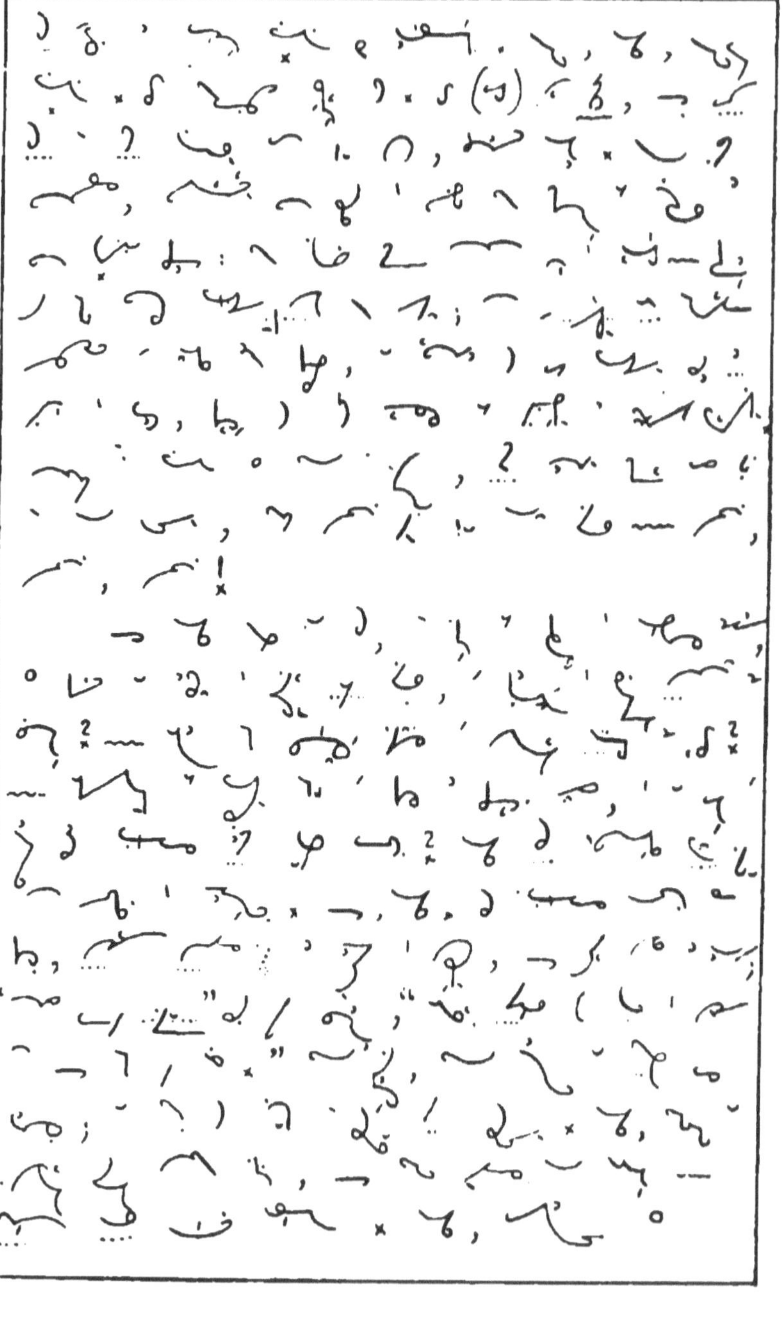

[shorthand text]

A sketch of the History of Shorthand

(Key on page 12 v.)

[shorthand text]

1588

"Characterie"

5)

16)

17)

200

JONES'S and *PITMAN'S interlined.*

(Key: — the last paragraph on page 11.)

J [shorthand symbols]

P [shorthand symbols]

J [shorthand symbols]

P [shorthand symbols]

J [shorthand symbols]

P [shorthand symbols]

J [shorthand symbols]

P [shorthand symbols]

J [shorthand symbols]

P [shorthand symbols]

J [shorthand symbols]

P [shorthand symbols]

J [shorthand symbols]

P [shorthand symbols]

J [shorthand symbols] "

P [shorthand symbols] "

(The above is written in accordance with Mr. Pitman's
10th Edition, as the alterations for the intended 11th
edition are not yet settled, the powers of many of the
consonant signs, having, of late, been changed
almost weekly, in the Phonetic Journal.)

1862.   J. B. De Voto & Co. Lithographers, GLASGOW.